Cambridge Elements

Elements in Music and the City
edited by
Simon McVeigh
University of London
Laudan Nooshin
City University, London

MAPPING (POST)COLONIAL PARIS BY EAR

Naomi Waltham-Smith
University of Warwick

CAMBRIDGE
UNIVERSITY PRESS

Shaftesbury Road, Cambridge CB2 8EA, United Kingdom

One Liberty Plaza, 20th Floor, New York, NY 10006, USA

477 Williamstown Road, Port Melbourne, VIC 3207, Australia

314–321, 3rd Floor, Plot 3, Splendor Forum, Jasola District Centre,
New Delhi – 110025, India

103 Penang Road, #05–06/07, Visioncrest Commercial, Singapore 238467

Cambridge University Press is part of Cambridge University Press & Assessment,
a department of the University of Cambridge.

We share the University's mission to contribute to society through the pursuit of
education, learning and research at the highest international levels of excellence.

www.cambridge.org
Information on this title: www.cambridge.org/9781009054652

DOI: 10.1017/9781009053921

First published 2023

A catalogue record for this publication is available from the British Library.

ISBN 978-1-009-05465-2 Paperback
ISSN 2633-3880 (online)
ISSN 2633-3872 (print)

Cambridge University Press & Assessment has no responsibility for the persistence
or accuracy of URLs for external or third-party internet websites referred to in this
publication and does not guarantee that any content on such websites is, or will
remain, accurate or appropriate.

Mapping (Post)colonial Paris by Ear

Elements in Music and the City

DOI: 10.1017/9781009053921
First published online: June 2023

Naomi Waltham-Smith
University of Warwick

Author for correspondence: Naomi Waltham-Smith, naomi.waltham-smith
@warwick.ac.uk

Abstract: What does the urban (post)colonial condition sound like? To what extent and how is France's colonial history audible today on the streets, specifically in the Parisian *quartiers populaires*? Musical and sonic production has long been entangled with social movements in France and its overseas territories, and genres such as hip hop and *raï* have been closely associated with the urban spaces of Paris's racialized neighborhoods and with political resistance. This Element refines and extends these analyses up to contemporary anti-racist and environmental struggles. Its novelty lies in telling these narratives from the perspective of the urban field recordist, reinventing the bourgeois figure of the *flâneur* as a feminist-decolonial activist and configuring listening as an expressly spatial practice of mapping the city. The discrete binaural microphones tucked in her ears capture everything from Franco-Maghrebi musical dissent through the sounds of police brutality and carceral capitalism to transcolonial reverberations with struggles elsewhere.

Keywords: sound, politics, postcolonial, Paris, field recording

ISBNs: 9781009054652 (PB), 9781009053921 (OC)
ISSNs: 2633-3880 (online), 2633-3872 (print)

Contents

1 The Voice of the (Post)colony: Radio, Hip Hop, and Soundscapes of the Street

"Va t'faire niquer, toi et tes livres." *Fuck you and your books!* This hostile apostrophe, hurled at legitimate culture with all the contempt of the *tutoiement*, is rapped by Booba on Lunatic's 2001 track "Hommes de l'ombres." Like much of Lunatic's output, it will likely be heard as imitating the codes of American gangsta rap with its tendency to celebrate money and violence.[1] The track flaunts its flight from social criticism into reactive materialism and asserts its autonomy while confessing to the commercialism that grants it the imprimatur to speak as the recognized voice of sociopolitical resistance. In this single sonic fragment there are multiple voices and audiences, multiple modes of address interacting with one another. These overlapping, conflicting interpellations made *in* sound – but also made *of* sound as it is called upon to *speak for* something – make it complicated to assign a voice to the (post)colonial without profound ambivalence or contradiction.

Certainly a book of the kind addressed by Booba – especially one written by a white scholar and published by an esteemed university press in the Global North – cannot give voice to that condition, and nor should it aspire to. But it can reflect critically on the complex and entangled mechanisms by which some sounds come to be heard as the voice of the (post)colonial in the context of France, its overseas territories, and the complex relation to its expansionist histories. It goes without saying that there is no single sound that stands in for this voice, which is necessarily multiple and fragmented, and yet there are a number of sounds that vie for that position or that, in particular moments and places, are elevated into that position, contingently hegemonizing the crisscrossed weave of a polyvocal sonic field. It would be easy to reduce the sound of the *banlieues* to the sounds of violence, gray economies, barbarity, alienation, delinquency, or, conversely those of resistance, rage, jubilation, passion, irrationality – each an element of the *banlieue*'s mediatized representation. They are all containers that restrict the dispersal and differentiation of sonic resonance in (post)colonial Paris.

The formulation in this section's title – the voice of the (post)colony – is therefore as fraught with unease as the prefix around which those parentheses hover, almost morphing into scare quotes. Both the voice and the "post" share a certain fragility and instability. The parentheses stubbornly refuse to evaporate because colonial forms of oppression and marginalization continue to persist today, these social relations turned inward and projected onto racialized populations within the Hexagon, in particular onto the Black and Arab children and

---

[1] The track can be heard online: www.youtube.com/watch?v=k_GrIMRijHU.

grandchildren of immigrants who live in the *banlieues*. This "post" is thus multidimensional and ambivalent, pointing to what comes after colonialism – simultaneously both as that which derives from it belatedly, and hence persists and remains of it, and as that which (largely in fantasy) supersedes, exceeds, and escapes that horizon. The German equivalent *nach*, which means both "after" and "according to," captures this double sense by which the *(post)*colonial is what follows from and in the wake of colonialism and from within that horizon envisions a future-to-come in which the chains of those lingering parentheses might at last be lifted. I take the "post" to articulate the multiple registers of vigilance that Christina Sharpe evokes with the phrase "in the wake": a vigil for the victims and losses of colonial violence, what comes to pass in the water behind the slave ship and continues to haunt the present, and the awakening to injustice and political consciousness.[2] In contrast with the foresight of vision, sound, insofar as it takes the form of wave and is propagated through resonant referral, is always somewhat *behind itself* – coming from all around including from behind, catching us by surprise and also marked by a belated syncopation (*nachträglich*).

In recent years France has witnessed an intensification of racialized marginalization, Islamophobia, and anti-immigrant sentiment in a *droitification* of political and media elites who have mainstreamed far-right views and persisted in denials of structural racism as an imported American concept irrelevant to French republican universalism. If, like anti-Blackness, colonialism is "interminable," there can be no straightforward mourning, memorialization, or veneer of repair for violence consigned to the past, for it is a death knell that continues to echo for Black and Arab men in the *cités*.[3] Françoise Vergès writes with reference to the work of French-Algerian artist and founder of the decolonial art and social space ~~La Colonie~~, Kader Attia, who grew up in the northeast Parisian *département* of Seine-Saint-Denis and whose hyphenated identity is erased by Eurocentric universalism: "For humiliation to be overcome, for wounds to heal, the injuries must first be shown and their histories *listened to*."[4] Aurality nurtures an awakening to psychoanalyst Karima Lazali's "blank space" of colonial trauma,[5] to the silenced tomb or crawlspace of the archive lyrically described in different ways by Harriet Jacobs, Saidiya Hartman, Katherine McKittrick, and Fred Moten.[6]

Resonating with the fugitivity of the Black radical tradition, to be "in the wake" of colonialism would therefore mean to be not only in the sights or

---

[2] Sharpe, *In the Wake*.   [3] Ibid., 19.
[4] Vergès, "Fire, Anger and Humiliation," 87 (emphasis mine).   [5] Lazali, *Le trauma colonial*.
[6] Jacobs, *Incidents in the Life of a Slave Girl*; Hartman, "Venus in Two Acts"; McKittrick, *Demonic Grounds*; Moten, *Black and Blur*. On the aurality of the crawlspace, see also Crawley, "Harriet Jacobs Gets a Hearing."

crosshairs of an entrenched colonial imaginary but also in a "line of flight."[7] For Sharpe it means both to inhabit and to rupture the colonial situation. Like a sound wave, the wake disturbs and sets ripples running across the surface. As such, the *banlieue*, fashioned as a mental – and often specific- ally a sonic – image by the circulation of mediatized stereotypes, is an echo of colonial violence but one that thereby retains the potential to rebound and ricochet otherwise, if belatedly. Listening is a practice of infinite repair tuning into the muted frequencies of colonial trauma – both militant and gentle.[8]

The voice, too, sits athwart persistent domination and infinite liberation, betwixt subjection and empowerment, highlighting their irreducible entangle- ment and incessant negotiation. The voice may be an instrument of colonial power that commands, instructs, enjoins, dismisses, silences but it is also the support for an incipient power to speak up or speak back: the cry of despair, the shouted demand, the rallying summons. To have a voice is already to be at least partially liberated from domination or to have the power at least to renegotiate the striated field of audibility that decides whose voice is heard more or less loudly, with more or less distortion. Sound production and reproduction – from the radio to noisy protest in the streets – have to this day played an important role in these processes in the French context, working at times to "flip the script" of who is heard and who gets to speak *for* particular communities or interests. This Element, together with its digital archive of field recordings and photo- graphs, aims to lend an ear to and sound with, resonate with, this sonic world, and as such to put itself in the wake of that tradition as a solidary reverberation. It aspires to a wakeful attunement, ears pricked with care-ful attention to the strains of coloniality's disturbances.[9] To this end, the Element oscillates between accounts of Paris's (post)colonial sounds and sonic ecologies, analyses of their sociopolitical contexts,[10] and critical reflections on listening as a method forged in those settings, especially in tandem with practices of walking and mapping.

---

[7] Sharpe, *In the Wake*, 18.

[8] I refer to the gentleness described by philosopher and psychoanalyst Anne Dufourmantelle in *Puissance de la douceur*.

[9] When I speak of care, I am thinking not only of Dufourmantelle but also of Vergès' decolonial analytic of care as reparation for what was laid to waste in racial and ecological devastation (*Un féminisme decolonial*) as well as the praxis, at the porous boundaries of theory and activism, of Madrid-based feminist collective Precarias a la Deriva ("A Very Careful Strike").

[10] On the longer history of the racialized *tumulte noir* in the Parisian and wider Francophone context: Hill, *Black Soundscapes, White Stages*; Gillett, *At Home in Our Sounds*; Moore, *Soundscapes of Liberation*.

In "Hommes de l'ombre" Booba raps, "ne reçoit d'ordre / ni des keufs / ni des profs." Refusing to take orders from the cops or his teachers, the rapper decries the authoritarian potential of the sonic address. Frantz Fanon describes how the French broadcasting station Radio-Alger suffused the colony with nostalgic reverberations of the metropole to reassure the settler of his civilized status, functioning as a sonic tether or dam against the threat of "Arabization."[11] Fanon observes that while the radio was a fixture in most French households in Algeria, the colonized, of whatever class, had little interest in a mouthpiece of the occupier addressed to French ears – an indifference that Fanon argues cannot simply be ascribed to the standard sociological explanation of an untranslatable culture but must take account of the distinctive psychopolitical dynamics of colonial domination of which the radio is a technological extension.[12] Michael Allan finds in Fanon's essay "a remarkable phenomenology of perception" that blends textual reading and embodied sensory perception beyond hermeneutics.[13] Fanon's account moreover implies that the entire apparatus of listening, not only the device itself, is a colonial prosthesis that technologizes the colonized subject in an "anxiogenic" reaction formation, "the voice of the oppressor" "not received, deciphered, understood but rejected" as hostile, accusatory, and inquisitory and putting the listener on guard.[14] Such anxious listening has already dislocated the self-identical and self-possessed subject of phenomenology in a way that implicates the temporal disjointedness and belatedness of the *(post)*-colonial.

A gradual uptake of radios would follow as the political situation evolved with the first stirrings of Tunisian independence in 1951–2, the Casablanca Uprisings and subsequent popular unrest in Morocco, and the start of Algeria's own war of independence with the declaration of the Front de Libération Nationale (FLN) addressed to the Algerian people on November 1, 1954, during which period the appetite for news from democratic media sources steadily grew. But radio consumption rose dramatically, Fanon recounts, with the announcement in late 1956 of a "Voix de l'Algérie Libre" (Voice of Free Algeria) that would bring other voices besides that of the oppressor – the voices of anti-colonial resistance and the revolution – to all Algerians, radically reconfiguring the radio and the entire prosthestic structure of colonial listening.

What is most striking is that, in Fanon's account, the incipient liberation and decolonization of the radio voice entails that its authoritative status be dispersed through the invention of techniques of listening and re-sounding. Prior to the emergence of la Voix de l'Algérie Libre, the radio served to amplify the telephonic address of the omnipotent voice of God, of the university, of the *Führer* –

---

[11] Fanon, "Ici la voix de l'Algérie," 307/71–72.   [12] Arnall, *Subterranean Fanon*, 121–22.
[13] Allan, "Old Media/New Futures": 188.   [14] Fanon, "Ici la voix de l'Algérie," 323/89.

in short, of the dominator – as European philosophers variously describe it. If for Sartre the radio listener is an inert object of the interpellating broadcast and for Adorno their autonomy is liquidated, for Jacques Derrida, reading Nietzsche, phonographic listening shares the university's goal of producing "docile and unquestioning functionaries" who, in "a ruse of the State," mistakenly believe themselves to enjoy total autonomy.[15] Derrida elaborates, referring to Nipper, the dog that became the iconic emblem of record label HMV (His Master's Voice).

> The hypocritical hound whispers in your ear through his educational systems, which are actually acoustic or acroamatic devices. Your ears grow larger and you turn into long-eared asses when, instead of listening with small, finely tuned ears and obeying the best master and the best of leaders, you think you are free and autonomous with respect to the State. You open wide the portals [*pavilions*] of your ears to admit the State, not knowing that it has already come under the control of reactive and degenerate forces. Having become all ears for this phonograph dog, you transform yourself into a high-fidelity receiver.[16]

Instead of this telephonic listening that tethers the listener via a leash or umbilical cord to the state and mandates a totalizing sameness, Derrida ponders a differentiation and prostheticization of listening that must come from the ear, or multiple ears, of the other.[17] Extending this to sexual difference, Derrida also quips in passing that there is here "no woman or trace of woman" (*pas de femme*) aside from the maternal.[18] The coupling of decoloniality and feminism inflects the modality of listening cultivated in this Element as *flânerie* undergoes deconstruction.

Something like this splintering or shattering of listening is already at work in Fanon's text. The French authorities swiftly began to jam the free voice, rendering it inaudible and forcing it constantly to jump frequencies, and the person in the room operating the radio, ear glued to the receiver, would be called upon to relay the voice as listeners struggled to tune into these fragmented, darting sounds. Decoding the crackle with accuracy was less important than the spontaneous, collaborative creation of narratives about the battles and combatants behind the static, which forged a collective consciousness attentive to difference, rather than the totalizing and essentializing unity of the colonial community. The effect was to produce a series of sonorous reticulations in which "every Algerian . . . wanted to become a reverberating element of the vast network of meanings born of the liberating combat."[19]

Ian Baucom makes the bold argument that Fanon, besides writing about the radio, turns texts like *Peau noire, masques blanc* into radiophonic listening

---

[15] Adorno, "On the Fetish-Character"; Sartre, *Critique of Dialectical Reason*, 270; Derrida, *Otobiographies*, 104/33.

[16] Derrida, *Otobiographies*, 107/34–35.   [17] Ibid., 107–9/35–36.   [18] Ibid., 118/38.

[19] Fanon, "Ici la voix de l'Algérie," 328/94.

devices. In his thinking "solidarity is antiphony, a technique of call and response, of listening and retransmitting."[20] Gavin Arnall highlights how anti-colonialism in Fanon's conception is not a reactive negation of domination that leaves its logic of assimilation intact but dismantles it through differentiation.[21] Similarly, Baucom stresses the need to scatter those sounds that have gathered a community of listeners. Hearing Paul Gilroy's study of diasporic sound-system culture as a differential "rebroadcast" of Fanon, Baucom proposes that listening is what traverses the gaps in transmission – the crackling, frequency-hopping radio signal and, metonymically, the traumatic cadences and foreclosures of the archive. Listening thereby forges the kind of local and translocal solidarities across struggles explored in Section 7.

In the *quartiers populaires* of Paris and other French cities, where immigrants from the former colonies and their descendants struggle to resist the exclusionary totalization of republican universalism, one might expect the "battle of the airwaves" (*guerre des ondes*) of the Algerian Revolution to find its ongoing reverberation in diasporic radio. A station such as Radio Beur (later Beur FM) was the voice of "Les Marches des Beurs" in 1983, which marked the emergence of a *beur* movement in the 1980s and has since continued critically to articulate transcolonial solidarities between the *banlieue* and the broader geographical space of the Maghreb. However, the role of its most prominent genre, *raï*, has followed a more accommodating course of politicizing sound than la Voix de l'Algérie Libre. Since the 1930s *raï* had thematized the social concerns of Algeria's Indigenous peoples alongside more lightweight topics, but its political force came to be blunted largely on account of its social liberalism, which meant that it formed part of the youth culture that reacted against anti-colonial Arab nationalism and, in its pop variant, would rapidly be recruited into a progressive acoustic hybridity friendly to the sensibilities of the Global North. In promoting its cross-fertilization with other genres, including funk, hip hop, R&B, and jazz, and in its appeals to mainstream cosmopolitan audiences, Beur FM's programming negotiated (post)colonial identities within the metropole, cultivating a cultural *métissage* that drew on the diverse *fond sonore* of the *cités* to deconstruct straightforward oppositions between ethnic difference and republicanism,[22] but increasingly this hybridity tended toward assimilating the former into the latter. As SOS-Racisme, an organization with close ties to the mainstream center-left Parti Socialiste but little popular support in the *quartiers*, began to sponsor multicultural concerts platforming *raï* in the 1980s, this cemented its more

---

[20] Baucom, "Frantz Fanon's Radio": 34.   [21] Arnall, *Subterranean Fanon*, 128–29.
[22] This formulation, which belongs to French-Congolese rapper and spoken-word artist Abd Al Malik, is quoted in Silverstein, "A Transnational Generation," 295.

integrationist status and Beur FM likewise became a paragon of assimilation, earning it a place among the *beurgeoisie*.[23]

It is to another musical genre associated with the *banlieue* – one that has perhaps even become *the* soundtrack of the *cités* – that one must turn to find a more intense reconfiguration of Fanon's "sound-wave warfare," as the English translation has it: Francophone hip hop and perhaps especially in its transformations of rap battle codes.[24] The film *Banlieusards* (released to Anglophone audiences on Netflix in 2019 as *Street Flow*), written by the French rapper Kery James, who was born in Guadeloupe to Haitian parents, and codirected with Leïla Sy with a cameo as a boxing trainer from *La Haine* director Mathieu Kassovitz, would remain somewhat crude and naive in its depiction of life in the *quartiers*, its characters and narrative endorsing stereotypes of spaces of lawlessness, drug-dealing, masculinist violence, social challenges, and racist policing, were it not for the film's ingenious conceit. Its ten-minute set piece, before a predictably tragically violent final act, cinematically translates the rap duel and specifically the address made to the state in James's 2012 track "Lettre à la République" into a formal debate in the *Concours d'éloquence* between studious Black *banlieusard* Souleyman Traoré, who is determined to avoid his older brother's local-celebrity lifestyle of money, drugs, and crime and to keep their younger brother out of trouble, and Lisa Crèvecœur, his fellow law student and love-interest, who is white and from the affluent *5ème arrondissement* in central Paris. That this display of oratory is an elevation of a rap battle has escaped most film critics, as has its metareflection on James's attempts to claim his own place within the French linguistic tradition, for instance in the 2008 "Banlieusards" in which he raps, "Regarde moi, j'suis noir et fier de l'être / J'manie la langue de Molière, j'en maîtrise les lettres."[25] Up for debate is the state's exclusive responsibility for the conditions in the *banlieues*. Lisa offers an ultimately paternalist sociological analysis of the causes of poverty and marginalization that leaves the *banlieusards* victims, dependent on the largesse of the state, and without agency – all, so he fires back, to absolve white guilt. In response, after calling him, in Malcolm X's term, a "house negro" to gasps from the floor, she recites a list of the Black and Arab men who have died at the hands of the police – Zyed and Bouna, Ali Ziri, Adama Traoré – and makes impassioned denunciations of the state's responsibility for racial violence and the oligarchization of democracy.

---

[23] Gross, McMurray, and Swedenburg, "Arab Noise and Ramadan Nights"; Echchaibi, "The Limits of French Universalism: Beur FM and Assimilation through Difference," in *Voicing Diasporas*, 75–122.

[24] Fanon, "Ici la voix de l'Algérie," 320/85.

[25] On this song and its music video's bid for recognition, see Dotson-Renta, "'On n'est pas condamné l'échec'": 356–57.

Souleyman furiously rejects the disempowerment to which such victimization condemns him, preferring to be a "soldier." It is an unsubtle analysis, more interesting when heard as a reflexive critique of rap's role in reproducing all these objectifying clichés. Calling her out for presuming to speak *for* the *banlieusards* and allowing her own rage to upstage theirs,[26] he delivers a devasting blow to hip hop and to every sonic construction of the *banlieue*, including those discussed in this Element and created through its research: "Je ne suis pas contenté de fantasmer la vie en banlieue et d'en déformer la réalité à travers objectif d'un appareil photo. La banlieue, je la connais" (I have never been content to fantasize about life in the suburbs, to deform the reality with the lens of a camera. The *banlieue* – I know it). This scene is helpful in pointing critically to how sonic production participates in constructing mythic images of *la banlieue* (in a reified singular), as dissected by Mame-Fatou Niang in the context of media discourses, cinema, and literature.[27] Whereas Niang aims to replace these images with the everyday normality of women's lives in the *quartiers* told from their standpoint, the research presented in this Element, including my own fieldwork in Paris, does not shy away from the extraordinary, the exceptional, the fabricated. It seeks to turn a critical ear (and lens) toward the process by which the (post)colonial city is represented sonically, how the racialized peripheries appear to the white core, especially when *la banlieue* comes to the center of Paris.

The Element aims expressly to thematize how the (post)colonial condition is rendered audible to – and is (mis)heard by – white civilizational-feminist ears and, working from this positionality and putting it into deconstruction, into the mode of a conditional, to begin to dismantle the schemas it traffics insofar as they marginalize, stigmatize, exoticize, fetishize, colonize. As I set out in Sections 2 and 5, this aural abolitionism entails finding new ways of moving through and mapping urban space that resist totalizing representations and at micro scales reconfigure the spatial dialectic of right and lawlessness into something more muscular, intimate, and carnal, with the intervening Sections 3 and 4 exploring the terrain in its borderings and mappings before turning in Sections 6 and 7 to counter-strategies for flipping their scripts through anti-fascist and decolonial-feminist praxis.[28] These modalities of moving

---

[26] Myisha Cherry gives an instructive warning to allies on the potential misuses of their anger, however well intentioned, in "Rage Renegades: A Special Message to 'Allies,'" in *The Case for Rage*, 118–38.

[27] Niang, *Identités françaises*.

[28] The idea, itself become an orthodoxy, that rap could be a "counterhegemonic" challenge to "dominant discourses," albeit entangled with contradictory processes of legitimation, was articulated by Tricia Rose in *Black Noise*, 102–3.

through the city mobilize the prosthetic articulations of aurality to unsettle relations between core and periphery.

This is not a text about hip hop or indeed about *music* specifically but about the wider category of *sound*. There is not space to do justice to the richness of the French scene in its musical or its sociopolitical complexity – a task that others have ably assumed.[29] Hip hop, *raï*, and other musical genres feature to the extent that they form a recognizable indexical component of the (post) colonial sonic environment in the city, much as African American hip hop has commodified racialized ghettoes in the United States.[30] The tension between the material conditions of hip hop's consumption and the social conditions it frequently thematizes and deplores as a performance of resistance is discussed in Section 6 in counterpoint with the circulation struggles of the *gilets jaunes*. Musical production is situated within a broader sonic ambience or atmosphere, mingling speech, live and recorded musics, noise pollution, everyday disturbances, and the sounds of protest, resistance, and flight – all forged in the crucible of ongoing colonialism. In Section 3 I analyze these atmospheres as "soundstates of emergency" to capture how the colonial state presupposes a savage exteriority – mere noise – that is yet to be civilized, universalized, and as such represents a category of rupture and disruption. In contrast to a fictionalized savagery, whether in its Macronist or Lepenist forms, I follow Louisa Yousfi in seeking out where sound expresses a vital and intimate barbarism that remains uncultured, untameable, irrecuperable beyond acculturation or integration. It is not in *rap conscient*, which continues to address itself to the state, but in the music of Booba or PNL that Yousfi finds a "oui et alors?" (and so what?) whose affirmation uproots Eurocentric logics of recognition and legibility, along with its literary and musical canons.[31]

The aim in submitting these sound ecologies to scholarly scrutiny is not to domesticate, civilize, or universalize them but to engage in a practice of *sounding with* the (post)colonial to make it resonate to the point where it shatters like a glass made to vibrate at its signature frequency. I proposed this notion of *shatter* in an earlier book while keeping its abolitionist impulse in reserve, but here this militant, even violent, species of resonance provides an analytic for making sense of sounds of/as counterviolence and of aurality's role in abolition democracy's dismantling of oppressive regimes and building of new institutions. Insofar as it arises immanently from being made to resonate with itself, *shatter* names less a frontal assault or radical elsewhere than an

---

[29] For example, Rollefson, *Flip the Script*; Durand (ed.), *Black, Blanc, Beur*; McCarren, *French Moves*.

[30] For this analogy, see, for example, Horvath, "Postcolonial Noise," 291.

[31] Yousfi, *Rester barbare*.

undoing under the pressure of vibrational intensity.[32] The city of Paris becomes a site for such sonic work and for reassessing sound's imbrication in politics. Noisy protest is a privileged site for such investigation because it condenses the struggle over audibility in colonial forms of governmentality (though by no means the only site for this sound-wave battle). Big, angry *manifs* crisscross the city's geographical divides and are scenes in which the demands of social movements press on the limitations of those established representative organs of political voice, parties and elections. The accompanying archive of field recordings, presented at the limits of reading, is bookended by the presidential elections of 2017 and 2022 and by the outcry following the death of a young Black French-Malian man, Adama Traoré, at the hands of the police on his birthday on July 19, 2016, and the 30th birthday stolen from him, marked after six years of his sister Assa's indefatigable campaign against the intensified state and police violence over which Macron has since presided and which his second-round opponent threatened to unleash without restraint. The last word of the Element goes to the resonant solidarities that Le comité Adama is building for a future that would abolish those spectral hesitations around the (post)colonial. Every word is inscribed with the hope for *vérité et justice* for Adama and all those brutally silenced by colonial violence.

2 Walking the City: Aural *Flânerie* from Baudelaire to Trespass

Most of this Element was conceived and composed while walking, whether that be strolling through central London's parks and along its canals, snowshoeing up Alpine ascents in the Alto Adige, or marching in demonstrations along Parisian boulevards. Thinking, especially in its philosophical and contemplative varieties, has long held an affinity with walking: Frédéric Gros writes of the eighteenth-century French thinker of politics and music, for example:

> Rousseau claimed to be incapable of thinking properly, of composing, creating or finding inspiration except when walking. The mere sight of a desk and chair was enough to make him feel sick and drain him of all courage. It was during long walks that the ideas would come, on the road that sentences would spring to his lips, as a light punctuation of the movement; it was paths that stimulated his imagination.[33]

Like Nietzsche, another musical thinker, my philosophical instincts had been sufficiently well schooled in the European tradition so as continuously to feel the urge to break free of the shackles of my desk and laptop, to which I would

---

[32] For Derrida's use of these aural metaphors to characterize what he calls "stricture," see *Negotiations*, 28–30.
[33] Gros, *Marcher*, 101/65.

return only hastily to type up the notes I had scribbled by hand in a notebook, perched on a park bench, or paused at a vantage point on a mountain trail. By force of habit, walking and philosophizing were happy bedfellows. Although I had been conducting fieldwork in Paris since the summer of 2013, it was only gradually that the methodology presented in this Element took shape, forged during a series of short trips to Paris and also in the course of anti-pipeline and anti-Trump protests in the United States in late 2016 before a sustained sabbatical in 2017 enabled me to submit my ambulatory inclinations to critically reflexive scrutiny on the streets on Paris. This meant interrogating the conditions for the liberation I enjoy and how, if they are denied to people of color in the *banlieues* whose political action is the subject of my study, my freewheeling peregrinations could be reconciled with a decolonial posture. If the philosopher-walker of German Romanticism – always a white cis man – were in his element on craggy Alpine or coastal trails, the endeavor would be to discover a rugged muscularity *dans la rue*, no longer in blissful yet bracing solitude but a walking-with that would be attuned to the obstacles and violence confronting Black and brown bodies and their self-defense without any naive pretense to identification or shared experience. This would mean acknowledging the irreducibility of the white intellectual's experience of walking in the city with its unhurriedness and its capacity for detachment, observation, and introspection, and reflecting on how the rhythms of walking-while-white structure ways of thinking and of knowing the world that obscure, erase, and even rationalize colonial power. This minimal ineradicable "shadow" cast by the fieldworker's colonialist position and its repertoires of walking, looking, and listening[34] lead to an immanent reflexivity that syncopates the surety of their footing without the fantasy of radical destruction, rupture, or escape – fantasies that risk obscuring the persistence of the (post)colonial.

Walking has long been associated with modes of thinking and reflecting, as both Gros and Rebecca Solnit show in their respective histories,[35] but, compared with, say, loafing, wandering, or meandering, walking is also said to bear a sense of stimulation, purpose, or waymaking in the world. In short, walking connects with commitment or action – something that ties together the otherwise different activities of pilgrimages and protest marches. Putting one foot in front of another is an engine that drives change – in the realm of ideas or politics. Such collective action politicizes the act of walking, as well as the thinking shaped by its cadences. Rather than reject outright inherited Eurocentric habits of walking, the methodology developed aims to allow these white-bourgeois templates to be deformed and gradually dismantled under the pressure of exposure to (post)colonial ways of navigating the city and of the force of

---

[34] Barz and Cooley (eds.), *Shadows in the Field.*   [35] Solnit, *Wanderlust.*

flânerie made to vibrate, beat against itself with discomfiting timbre, potentially to the point of shattering. In short, it involves embracing the plasticity of walking in the sense that Catherine Malabou uses the term to mean both malleability and explosive destruction.[36] To put it crudely: What effect does it have on the gait of the *flâneur* to fire Flash-Balls at their feet and what possibilities for walking-*with* the colonized are opened up or foreclosed?

The fact that women and people of color do not enjoy the same liberty to make their way through the city – or indeed, as read or reading, through the pages of philosophically inflected books such as this one – rebounds on the liberty of walking in general if walking as methodology – and likewise reading or what I will call readlistening – is to be sensitive to the otherwise calibrated relations to the city that spatial segregation creates. While Jacqueline L. Scott has shown the extent of racialized exclusion from walking in nature,[37] the focus here is on the distinct ways in which the freedoms associated with walking-in-the-wild are reserved to the white-bourgeois urban experience when the figures of Romanticism are transplanted to the city of modernity, of which Paris has been the quintessential expression. If the city was figured on this model as a "wilderness," as in Walter Benjamin's formulation "botanizing on the asphalt,"[38] it is its racialized or otherwise marginalized inhabitants who were othered as "savages," the mere fact of their walking in the city stigmatized or criminalized. Describing his experience in the United States, Garnette Cadogan, for example, writes:

> Walking while black restricts the experience of walking, renders inaccessible the classic Romantic experience of walking alone. It forces me to be in constant relationship with others, unable to join the New York flâneurs I had read about and hoped to join. Instead of meandering aimlessly in the footsteps of Whitman, Melville, Kazin, and Vivian Gornick, more often I felt that I was tiptoeing in Baldwin's . . . Walking as a black man has made me feel simultaneously more removed from the city, in my awareness that I am perceived as suspect, and more closely connected to it, in the full attentiveness demanded by my vigilance. It has made me walk more purposefully in the city, becoming part of its flow, rather than observing, standing apart.[39]

Much ink has also been spilt on whether women can join these ranks – can there be *flâneuses*? – considering the equation made between women's visibility, from the spectacle of the promenade in public gardens to the stigmatized "walk of shame" and streetwalking, and sexual availability.[40] Christina

---

[36] Malabou, *L'avenir de Hegel*.   [37] Scott, "Do White People Dominate the Outdoors?"
[38] Benjamin, "The Paris of the Second Empire," 19.   [39] Cadogan, "Walking While Black."
[40] Solnit, *Wanderlust*, chapter 14; Elkin, *Flâneuse*; Nesci, *Le flâneur et les flâneuses*; Parsons, *Streetwalking in the Metropolis*.

Horvath asks if it is possible to be a *flâneuse* in the *banlieues*, assuming that anyone could *flâner* in this urban setting where distances are much greater, residential and commercial zoning are more distinctly separated, and streets less densely packed. Horvath argues that the women and girls of color who live in these neighborhoods are stereotypically confined to private, domestic spaces indoors or walking for clearly circumscribed purposes such as going to school or grocery shopping, whereas street corners, stairs, entrances to buildings, and rooftops from which they can observe the world are the preserve of men and boys.[41] To the extent that gender segregation and divisions of labor regulate walking in the *quartiers* – and arguably it is overstated in the sociological literature insofar as it reproduces well-worn images of Franco-Maghrebi men as drug dealers, rioters, terrorists, and Islamists whose conceptions of women do not measure up to Western liberal-bourgeois feminist standards – it is compounded by the racial carving up of space that delegitimizes both their presence in the center of Paris and their leisured movements.

Notwithstanding these considerable challenges, I do not see the figure of the *flâneur*, itself a far from homogeneous but diverse and evolving category, as entirely bankrupt, if only because the archetype continues to inform the minimal conditions of my walking in the city, as a white intellectual of (acquired) middle-class standing. Likewise the practices of technologically mediated listening adopted retain indelible traces of the field recorder's colonial history as an instrument of cultural (dis)appropriation and surveillance. I am interested in how the streets of Paris – the city in which it became possible and indeed fashionable to inhabit the alienation of modern industrialized capitalism but which also has a venerable tradition of treating its streets and public squares as arenas for democratic action and assertions of the right to the city – might become the crucible for unravelling and chipping away at the posture of *flânerie* and of recording as the wanderer or traveler's tool for making the other collectible via a combined dismantling of patriarchy, colonialism, and the imperialism of the senses.

Having determined that I wanted to see what environmental sound as a whole, rather than stories, interviews, or other first-person accounts, what sound *speaking for itself*, could tell us about (post)colonial Paris, the decision to focus on the deconstruction of *flânerie* was made in conjunction with one to record at marches, demonstrations, and skirmishes typically, though not exclusively, in central Paris, instead of during perambulations around the *quartiers populaires* where the comparative lack of conditions of anonymity and publicity would urge sliding into a more ethnographic mode of encounter. There were reasons to prefer the movement of walking over the in situ time-lapse recordings

---

[41] Horvath, "Quelle place pour les flâneuses."

with which I had initially experimented in that they better captured the mapping and countermapping of the city that I discuss in Section 4. Rather than how the *banlieues* sound on the ground or from Paris itself, maintaining the border between center and periphery, the recordings seek to chart how the *quartiers* sound when they come to, impress on, and assert their audibility within the imperial core. There is transgressive, border-crossing power in racialized citizens and the *sans papiers* marching and making noise not only in Beaumont-sur-Oise, for example, but also in the symbolic spaces of power from which they are excluded, as they did in June 2020 in resonance with Black Lives Matter protests against the murder of George Floyd in the United States or in April 2022 at a manifestation *contre l'extrême droite et ses idées* [Audio 1].[42]

Notwithstanding its problematic panoptical and panacoustical character which threatens partially to reproduce the police state, the figure of the *flâneur*, its variants, descendants, and *doppelgänger* offer a reservoir of techniques upon which to draw, especially diversifying its sensory dimensions to break down a class-inflected hierarchy of the senses led by an elite, male "disembodied eye."[43] In their Walking Lab project, Stephanie Springgay and Sarah E. Truman note that "walking methodologies invariably invoke sensory, haptic, and affective investigations."[44] While the French eighteenth- and nineteenth-century sources vary on whether it is predominantly "the gastronomy of the eye" (*la gastronomie de l'œil*) in Balzac's well-known phrase or more multisensory,[45] *flânerie* has commonly been defined by both heightened sensory acuity and the liberty of remaining detached from the crowd in which the *flâneur* moves. Even if the mass of demonstrators is not the crowd that Baudelaire, Balzac, Fournel, or Benjamin contemplated, the notion of *flânerie* captures something of the sensory orientation of my research and the irreducibility of the observer status in my participation and hence of the colonizer's disposition in ethnographic practice on account of its genealogy. When walking while recording, I am neither straightforwardly a demonstrator (no matter what sympathies I might have for the cause or however impelled I might feel to join in the chants) nor a photojournalist (even if I sometimes walk backward in step with the press pack ahead of the march) nor a sociologist collecting data on protest repertoires and morphologies (even if I am interested in the traces that tactics or the composition of the crowd leave in the sound). Following protests remotely via live video streams during the pandemic also brought home how, in an age of digital mediatization in which protestors themselves garner global

---

[42] For further information on how to access the additional content of this Element please see the "Supplementary Material" section.

[43] See Boutin, "Rethinking the Flâneur": 126.

[44] Springgay and Truman, *Walking Methodologies*, 12.   [45] Cited in ibid., 124.

attention for their cause by posting photos and videos, my quasi-documentary approaches to photographing and recording were not straightforwardly of the order of surveilling, collecting, or fetishizing Black and brown bodies but tangential to the work of "engaged" journalists there to bolster dissemination (indeed I was often asked by protestors to take and share photos, and photos I took would be reposted on Instagram, including by Assa Traoré). The movement of my feet, ears, and camera lens were in a sense already choreographed in advance as a kind of invitation to solidary media dissemination.

My approach deliberately contrasts with and complements more collaborative participatory approaches that seek to diversify knowledge and perception and in which I have engaged in other projects. This fieldwork was designed to inscribe and thereby put pressure on the (post)colonial researcher's position. Unlike work in geography on decolonial cartographies that distinguishes the head-on anti-colonial assault, which leaves the colonial orientation intact, even affirmed, from the decolonial pluralization of mappings, which decenters Eurocentric spatial practices, I read the de- in decolonial through the detour of de-construction. Specifically, I follow in the wake of, without remaining faithful to, Derrida's deconstructive gesture as one that is deeply imbricated with sovereignty from the self to the state as a foundational principle of European thought and political life. The decolonial thinking that I follow here is *tout contre* colonialism: not so much totally against as pressed right up against it. Sovereignty cannot be destroyed by something other than (or after) sovereignty but only by other sovereignties. And yet, as he carefully distinguishes between "his" deconstruction and Jean-Luc Nancy's, this is not simply a question of multiplying, of saying that there is no one or "the" sovereignty but many, but of putting sovereignty in question under the sign of the conditional. In Derrida's syntagm "*s'il y en a*" (if there is such a thing), it is the very possibility of Eurocentric, metaphysical, colonial sovereignty that is opened up, not in a radical exit but in the possibility that *there might be no such thing.*[46] This, I would suggest, is not straightforwardly to leave the colonial subject center stage, though it does turn on the ungrounding and dismantling of that subject formation perhaps more than on the other forms of listening, seeing, and walking that come in its wake. To accept the impossibility of its erasure is not to bow to the colonial monument (it must still be seen falling into the dock) but to bear immanent witness to its ongoing violence.

This contradictory subject position is reflected in my recording techniques. The use of discrete in-ear binaural microphones, which produce a stereo image whose subtle interaural differences put the listener in the place of the recordist,

---

[46] Derrida, *Le toucher*, 323–24/287–88.

on the one hand gives a strikingly immersive sensory experience, with the sound almost becoming tactile and far more intimate with the crowd (*tout contre*) than the lavalier or shotgun mics typically used by the press corps, and on the other hand enables my act of sonic observation to go undetected (including by the police). This means that what I record and what I choose to retain and publish calls for an ethical responsibility at each moment if it is to keep watch *with* in the sense of a wake or vigil rather than surveillance or spectacle. I take my cue from Fred Moten's reading, via Hartman, of Édouard Glissant's right to opacity as a deconstruction of subjection/ivity in which her veiled Black sound becomes "the keeping of this secret even in the midst of its intensely public and highly commodified dissemination ... relayed and miscommunicated, misheard, and overheard, often all at once, in words and in the bending of words, in whispers and screams."[47] Derrida's arguments about dismantling sovereignty by exposing its contingency gives this overhearing a distinctive valence, a reverberant redoubling that syncopates the single totalizing vantage point of sovereignty, putting it out-of-joint spatially and temporally. This gesture, beyond simply pluralizing modes of listening that are known, disturbs the very exclusionary system according to which colonial-sovereign ways of listening continue to secure their hegemony even among a plurality of auralities.

My overhearing contrasts with my use of a full-frame DSLR camera to take candid photographs while recording, which means that I am anything but inconspicuous and will engage silently with the protestors in the split second in which they often turn to look into the lens and in the moment afterward when I confirm consent through a hand gesture, nod, or smile, drawing on the reservoirs of unspoken solidary recognition. I deliberately shoot with fast primes (wide-angle 24mm, 85mm portrait lens, and occasionally the street photographer's classic 50mm) to force me to move my feet to get the desired composition whether for portraiture or crowd shots [Photos 1–6. Photo 5 is a color version of Figure 1],[48] reveling in the traces of my movement (scurrying, weaving, crouching) in the field recordings. I am thus more mobile than the average protestor, often hastily moving up and down the length of the demonstration to capture the complex counterpoints between the chants of different political groups, dawdling to let it pass by me for a minute or so to take in the sonic diversity, or circling around a drumming band as they give a breathtaking thirty-minute performance warning of impending climate catastrophe [Audio 2].

In her reading of Balzac's *Physiologie du marriage*, Catherine Nesci argues that the *flâneur*, as physiognomist and musician, is able to decipher and

---

[47] Moten, *B Jenkins*, 105, referencing Hartman, *Scenes of Subjection*, 35–36 and Glissant, *Poétique de la relation*, 203–9/189–94.

[48] For further information on how to access the additional content of this Element please see the "Supplementary Material" section.

Figure 1 1ᵉʳ tour social, April 22, 2017, Boulevard du Temple

transform the disorganized and confused melee of street sounds into a "musical score."[49] Without aspiring to any naive fidelity, my recordings do not aim at the compositional or aesthetic synthesis that Boutin, for example, describes,[50] preferring to leave the whole a little blurry and undone, gesturing to the infrapolitics of lower frequencies to rework Paul Gilroy's phrase.[51] The recordings accompanying this Element are certainly framed but otherwise minimally edited (only to fix clipping), although I have also made bricolage-style sonic compositions, paired with still photographs, for gallery installations. Both approaches, in different ways, mine the ragpicking predilections of the *flâneur*'s forerunner, the *chiffonier*, who collects the discarded detritus and marginalia of everyday life like the fragments of seemingly trivial sound that prick up my ears around the edge of the protest chants and musical performances, as well as the montage techniques of the figure's surrealist successor. You are invited to listen to the audio clips while or in between reading, in or out of sequence, attentive or somewhat distracted, still or walking, to hear through colonizing ears put into a spin, but also to enjoy the polyvocality of the sonic textures, which are loosely tethered through narrative or image to a context, but without a dissecting analytical commentary that would prescribe how one hears – trying not to subject the violence one hears and the resistance it provokes to the redoubled violence of a reductive or masterful readlistening.

---

[49] Nesci, *Le flâneur et les flâneuses*, 114 (also cited in Boutin, "Aural Flânerie": 154).
[50] Boutin, "Aural Flânerie": 159.   [51] Gilroy, *The Black Atlantic*, 37.

If walking is an "amateur act" that "trespasses through everybody else's field" without alighting for long in any of them,[52] it is nevertheless necessary to do more than rove across the disciplines from anthropology to geography, literature to cultural history, gardening to urban design in order to develop critical walking methodologies that challenge racial and gender segregation of urban space. One way to do this might be via the subversive mobility of errant bodies moving out-of-place, taking inspiration from a trajectory of praxis inspired by the Situationist *dérive*. While the role of women in the Situationist movement has often been overlooked, women in cities have daily been remapping the geographical and psychic spaces of oppression, as Horvath examines, for example, in her study of female protagonists in *banlieue* fiction, who, she claims, surreptitiously evade male control, unlike the "Ni Putes Ni Soumis" (neither whores nor doormats) movement that she holds up as an example of collectively and assertively reclaiming public space.[53] I draw in part on the ruses of the *flâneuse*: androgynous dress, what look like headphones, face coverings.

However, it is necessary to question the extent to which drifting remains a liberal heteronormative practice that ultimately reproduces racial and class exclusions and demands to be queered and decolonized, taking its direction from notions of decolonial-feminist and Indigenous practice. Specifically addressing walking, Jasbir Puar, referring to Sara Ahmed's warning against a binary choice between assimilation and transgression through the fetishization of movement as freedom, argues that elite-cosmopolitan queerness, figured as transgression, constrains this deviance in relation to an often universalizing normativity, advocating instead for a critically reflexive stance toward intersectionality, unafraid to acknowledge its own conservativisms or complicities.[54] Horvath recognizes critiques of "Ni Putes Ni Soumis" and other narratives by which women in the *quartiers* are said to be rescued by an enlightened, state-sanctioned civilizational feminism from a sexism from below imposed on them by their husbands and brothers, although it is noteworthy that even this critique is advanced with the alibi of a white liberal feminist, Joan Scott, in her notion of "sexularism."[55]

Puar, following Saba Mahmood, cautions against valorizing a universal category of resistance. Mahmood's argument is incisive:

> I believe it is critical that we ask whether it is even possible to identify a universal category of acts – such as those of resistance – outside of the ethical and political conditions within which such acts acquire their particular meaning. Equally important is the question that follows: does the category of

---

[52] Solnit, *Wanderlust*, 4.   [53] Horvath, "Quelle place pour les flâneuses."
[54] Ahmed, *The Cultural Politics of Emotion*, 151–52; Puar, *Terrorist Assemblages*, 22–24.
[55] Fernando, *The Republic Unsettled*, 187.

resistance impose a teleology of progressive politics on the analytics of power – a teleology that makes it hard for us to see and understand forms of being and action that are not necessarily encapsulated by the narrative of subversion and reinscription of norms?[56]

Mahmood therefore urges the need to "problematize ... the universality of the desire – central for liberal and progressive thought, and presupposed by the concept of resistance it authorizes – to be free from relations of subordination and, for women, from structures of male domination." In the context of a republican normative, identitarian, and increasingly authoritarian conception of *laïcité* much in evidence in contemporary political debates in France, to which a liberal-democratic variant, rooted in the autonomy of civil society and individual liberty, appears as the only alternative, it is a matter of deconstructing – which is also to decolonize – the universal.[57] Walking or listening practices need not be adventurous or wayward, or at least not in imitation of the Eurocentric ideals of freedom that masquerade as ahistorical and universal, but are built "on the backs of the colonized."[58]

Preempting the themes to be discussed in greater detail in Section 7, Houria Bouteldja, a French-Algerian activist and, until October 2020, founding member and spokesperson of the Parti des Indigènes de la République (PIR), warns against trying to advance feminist liberation by pitting one patriarchy (white, imperialist, neoliberal) against another (Indigenous, from below, religious) without first dismantling the colonial domination by which state violence against Black and brown men ricochets onto women in the *quartiers*. Forging a path to common liberation, argues Bouteldja, invoking the metaphorics of wilderness walking, "would have to take the sinuous and craggy routes [*les voies sinueuses et escarpées*] of a paradoxical movement, which will necessarily have to pass through a communitarian allegiance. At least, so long as racism exists."[59]

Scholarship on soundwalking as a methodology, especially in an urban context, frequently characterizes practices of soundmaking or even of walking while listening in silence or to a composed audio track as ways to rescript, reclaim, reoccupy, or otherwise reappropriate public space.[60] In more extreme form, trespass can be a way to reclaim the commons from the dispossession of capitalist private property,[61] but, following Puar and Ahmed, not all are equally free to trespass. When human-rights lawyer Raja Shehadeh has walked over the years in

---

[56] Mahmood, *Politics of Piety*, 9–10.
[57] This has been an important theme in Étienne Balibar's work beginning with "Racism As Universalism."
[58] Bouteldja, *Les Blancs, les Juifs et nous*, 88/91.   [59] Ibid., 84/87.
[60] For example: Biserna, "Ambulatory Sound-Making."
[61] For example: Hayes, *The Book of Trespass*.

the hills of Ramallah – his mobility increasingly restricted by the occupation, expanding settlements, despoliation of land, and the division of the West Bank into three Zones putting open country out of bounds to Palestinians – his trespass is an act of resistance at considerable bodily risk.[62] But his *sarha*, a Palestinian and typically male practice of roaming freely and aimlessly, also has spiritual, testimonial, and memorial connotations, creating a palimpsest of erased places, lives, and cultures over the landscape, deep inner voyage, solidary bonds, and unexpected encounters, as well as radically transforming writing as a journey in itself. I adopt walking-with as a method in part because (philosophical) thought needs to go for a walk, to meander, to drift aimlessly, to trespass so that it might loosen its certainty, its definitive direction, purpose, and boundaries, and therefore become more open-minded, humble, patient, and courageous – that, in opening its ears, it might retune the universal "*à la mesure du monde.*"[63]

3 Soundstates of Emergency: Expressions of Bordering and Transgression

Underscoring the famous sequence in Gillo Pontecorvo's *La battaglia di Algeri* (1966) in which three female militants of the FLN prepare by cutting and dyeing their hair and by changing into European clothing to pass through checkpoints so they can plant bombs is the sound of *qarāqib* (metal crotales) against the pounding of the large, double-headed *tbel*. This distinctive sound of Gnawa drumming, which has its roots in the communities of sub-Saharan African brought to Morocco as slaves, returns intermittently throughout the sequence as the militants take delivery of the packages from the bomb-maker and as one of the women enters and later looks around the café. It resurfaces for a final time in the film's more hopeful closing scene in which a large crowd of demonstrators is yelling and some women ululating. Just as the camera zooms in on the faces of two vociferous Algerian women, the percussion enters, the diegetic shouting fading out as the camera briefly tracks the face of a young woman gesticulating excitedly with a flag and mouthing furiously at the police. As in the earlier sequence, the drumming serves to drown out or displace speech, rendering her remonstrations silent.

Drumming of various styles is a common feature in the field recordings I have made at protests in Paris. This recording [Audio 3] in particular, made at a demonstration in the *banlieue* neighborhood of Aubervilliers on April 16, 2017, has a similarly persistent and perhaps ominous quality as the film soundtrack, except that the drumming this time undergirds the shouting and

---

[62] Shehadeh, *Palestinian Walks*. See also Macfarlane, *The Old Ways*; Moore, *Narrating Postcolonial Arab Nations*, 193–211.

[63] Mame-Fatou Niang and Julien Suaudeau borrow this phrase from Aimé Césaire in their book *Universalisme*, 60.

Figure 2 Paris-banlieue contre le FN, April 16, 2017, Rue du Chemin de Fer

chanting, driving it forward. There are ways in which, I shall suggest, the vocal sounds here are also structurally silenced through the coarticulation. The sense of foreboding perhaps only comes retroactively, unlike in the film, in that it is within only a few minutes of the end of this recording that skirmishes begin to break out with the police on the approach past Porte de la Villette to Le Zénith arena where Marine Le Pen is due to hold a campaign rally the next day [Audio 4, Photo 7]. During the course of the persistent drumming, the procession passes first underneath the Périphérique that marks the administrative limits of Paris, dividing the city from the *banlieues*, here specifically marking the boundary between one of the most impoverished *départements* in France, Seine-Saint-Denis – *le 9–3* – and rapidly gentrifying parts of the *19ème arrondissement* and then under the railway tracks at Porte de la Villette [Photos 8–9. Photo 8 is a color version of Figure 2]. When the drumming restarts amid the exchanges of projectiles and a temporary lull in chanting, it sounds the presentiment of fascist violence [Audio 5, Photo 10].

This sonorous quasi-echo across a historical span of sixty years traces and sounds out the limits of boundaries between inside and outside, center and periphery, metropole and colony, place and non-place, law and anomie. As such I analyze both examples as "soundstates of emergency," adapting the name for the structure of governmentality extensively analyzed by Giorgio Agamben among others to suggest how sound is imbricated as a vital instrument and medium in the operation of law and sovereign power. The neologism is also intended as a distorted echo of the familiar term "soundscape" advanced by members of the World Soundscape Project and within the emerging domain of soundscape ecology, putting sound on the wider agenda for the humanities and social sciences. The concept has received considerable critical scrutiny, often due to what Marie Thompson criticizes as Murray Schafer's "aesthetic moralism," which reinforces the pathological stigmatization of noise in hygienist discourses on the city.[64] The term "soundstate," far from suggesting an ontologization of sound or a mythic state of nature, seeks to draw attention to the composed, fabricated character of the (post)colonial city's sonic worlds and to sound's entanglement in sociomaterial compositions that structure the city as a territory. Soundstate means the state of sound in the sense both of what state sound is in (how the distribution of audibility is composed at a given time and place through a field of sociopolitical forces) and as an apparatus of the state and its reach into people's everyday urban lives.

Writing "against soundscape," Timothy Ingold warns against turning sound into an object of playback rather than a medium of multisensory perception.[65] He complains that when we listen to our surroundings there is not already a soundscape that preexists our hearing. In making use of field recordings without accepting Schafer's sonic naturalism or turning them into a text, my research in Paris has been interested in what those recordings, as the minimally composed capture of sound, can reveal about the processes of composition of those soundstates such that the confident distinction between object and medium is challenged by the prosthetic articulation of listening as it transgresses and dismantles multiple boundaries between inside and outside, perception and cognition, noisy and faithful. Soundstates of emergency are, in short, attempts to contain the multifarious dissemination of sound and to marshal its force so as to demarcate and enforce divisions of exploitation and oppression. Soundstates are prototypically imperialist compositions and, given the crucial historical role played by field recording in producing them, the irreducibility of this apparatus – of listening *to* alongside *with* – is audible in the audio examples accompanying this Element. As Hill explicates, the imperial ear supplements the (dis)possessing imperial gaze, granting access to a sublime incommensurability exceeding the frontiers of dominant visual paradigms, thus extending the expansionist fantasy.[66] For all the confusion and disarray of aurality, a soundstate nonetheless produces a symbolic image of *la banlieue* within the logic of internalized colonialism – one that fixes to a point and thereby stigmatizes and silences, always (ex)appropriating the outside. For this reason, I suggest, soundstates are not simply to be fled in the direction of fetishizing

[64] Thompson, *Beyond Unwanted Sound.*   [65] Ingold, "Against Soundscape."
[66] Hill, *Black Soundscapes*, 2–8.

either sound's affect-laden materiality, its promiscuous movement, or its mute purity – which would reproduce empire's orientalizing gestures – but to be reckoned with as effective fictions that govern Paris's spatial politics. Like Hill, I am interested in how the redoubled beats of sound can reveal the incoherencies, failures, and slippages of colonial logic, unsettling the efficacy of its fictions.

Both sonic scenes, in 1957 and 2017, take place within an *état d'urgence*, whose recurrence and arguably ongoing persistence in colonized spaces over the course of French history garnered increasing attention after its invocation to curb the *banlieues* riots in 2005 and its normalization since the coordinated deadly attacks of November 13, 2015, in Paris and Saint-Denis.[67] The new law adopted on April 3, 1955, that inaugurated the French *état d'urgence*, Public Law 55-385, conferred broad police powers on the civil authorities in Algeria to restrict freedom of movement and assembly. It would operate only for eight months in the first instance, but related special powers allowing the French government to rule via executive orders would permit similar measures to be revived in practice at various points during the Algerian Revolution, including during those events depicted in the film. The *état d'urgence* would be in force for the first time in metropolitan France for a month in May 1958 to counteract a feared *coup d'état* by generals of the colonial army in Algeria. With the collapse of the Fourth Republic, Charles de Gaulle seized the opportunity to consolidate state power, including securing extraordinary presidential powers in the event of a threat to the Republic within Article 16 of the Constitution of the Fifth Republic.

De Gaulle invoked Article 16 on April 23, 1961, in response to an ultimately failed military operation in Algeria, known as the *Putsch de généraux*, that sought to force him not to relinquish control of the colony in the wake of a referendum on Algerian independence received overwhelming support – 75 percent of voters – in France. The *état d'urgence*, which aimed to prevent an ultimately shortlived coup from spreading to the metropole, nonetheless persisted for a much longer period.

In October 1961, in the context of what were heard as calls to incitement for revenge for FLN bombings against the police, Préfet de police de Paris Maurice Papon, who had a reputation for supervising the repression and torture of political prisoners in Algeria and would be for convicted for overseeing the deportation of Jews to Nazi Germany under the Vichy regime, imposed a curfew exclusively on Algerian Muslim workers, French Muslims of Algerian origin,

---

[67] Some accounts of the history of *l'état d'urgence*: Lambert, "Introduction: A Short Colonial History of the French State of Emergency"; Vergès, "State of Emergency"; Thénault, "L'état d'urgence"; Gaiser Fernandes, *Everyday State of Emergency*.

and French Muslims. Notwithstanding police raids and arrests, a sizable demonstration, around 30,000 strong, mobilized in the streets against the restrictions on the night of October 17. What followed was a massacre, though its recognition as such by the French state has been negligible. Police arrested around a third of the crowd, opened fire on demonstrators, and threw many into the Seine where they drowned. Historians estimate the number of people killed to have been between 200 and 300. In the years that followed Algerian independence, in which France continued to exercise greater or lesser control over a number of its colonies and administratively integrated territories, including those that remain to this day overseas territories (the *outre-mer*), the *état d'urgence* was deployed in 1985 as part of a violent settler-colonial apparatus to repress Indigenous dissent in Kanaky (named "New Caledonia"), in 1986 to coerce Indigenous representatives in Wallis and Futuna, and in 1987 in Tahiti and nearby Moorea to contain a dockers' strike that was escalating into unrest.

It would not be until November 2005 that the 1955 colonial law would be invoked again in the Hexagon in a bid to pacify the *banlieue* revolts in Paris and other urban areas after a Black and an Arab teenager, Bouna Traoré and Zyed Benna, died from electrocution on October 27 in Clichy-sous-Bois while attempting to hide in an electric substation to evade police who appeared to pursue them without good cause. As cars and buses burned and the air filled with the sounds of rage and with tear gas in the *banlieues*, the *état d'urgence* was extended on November 16 for a further three months. Minister of the Interior at the time Nicholas Sarkozy had fanned the flames with racist rhetoric when in June he had proposed "to hose down the projects" (*nettoyer au Kärcher la cité*) and just two days before the deaths he promised "to rid them of scum" (*débarasser de la racaille*). Alongside a huge deployment, the police had the power to determine which areas be subject to curfew, sometimes extending to the entirety of racialized proletarian population and not only the youth, thus highlighting once again the *spatial* exclusion at work in a state of emergency that reproduces and projects colonial and border regimes onto the spaces of the city. That this exemplified what Kawtar Najib calls "spatialized Islamophobia," projected systemically across global to infra-urban scales,[68] became hard to deny when the *état d'urgence* declared in November 2015 in order to counteract terrorism led to arrests and house searches that overwhelmingly targeted Muslims, constructing them as "the interior enemy" (*l'ennemi intérieur*).[69] The *état d'urgence* lasted for two years before large swathes of the measures were incorporated into the common law before its latest iteration with the

---

[68] Najib, *Spatialized Islamophobia*.
[69] Rigouste, *L'ennemi intérieur*; Mechaï and Hergon, "Make Yourself at Home!"

announcement of an *état d'urgence sanitaire* on March 23, 2020 that would be renewed for a second period in the Hexagon and would be especially prolonged in the *outre-mer* – where it may in part explain Marine Le Pen's notable cut-through in the second round of the 2022 presidential election to beat Emmanuel Macron in several territories that had overwhelmingly supported radical-left candidate Jean-Luc Mélenchon in the first round.

Thinking through the prism of the aesthetic and specifically the sonorous complicates regimes of representation that, via this historical thread of the *état d'urgence* with its reprise of the *Code d'Indigénat*, suture the logics and apparatuses of France's colonial past to the (post)colonial condition of the *banlieues* today. It moreover unsettles any positivist sociological determination of the "state" of affairs that risks "naturalizing racial difference in place."[70] The notion of an imperial boomerang effect, by which the colonized periphery rebounds upon on the core in the guise of marginalities of race and class, has been given different nuances, but thinking of sonic boomerangs or *renvoi* points to an aesthetic or poetic shattering of what sociopolitical empiricism seeks to stabilize and schematize. Both Aimé Césaire and Jean-Paul Sartre deploy the term "boomerang" to describe how colonial violence reverberates upon the colonizer either straightforwardly as retaliation or as dehumanization whereby "the habit of seeing the other man as *an animal* [*la bête*] ... treating him like an animal ... tends objectively to transform [even the most civilized man] himself *into an animal* [*en bête*]" – the *ensauvagement* of the colonizer, as it were, to redeploy a right-wing dog whistle embraced by ministers in Macron's government eager not to be outflanked by Le Pen, such as Gérald Darmanin, so as to stigmatize racialized descendants of migration.[71] Like Hannah Arendt, Césaire further sees another, slower boomerang effect by which European "civilization" descends into the barbarity of Nazism under the pressures of imperialist wars and repatriated colonial violence.[72] The term "imperial boomerang" has come chiefly to refer to this last element, whereby the export of European juridico-political apparatuses to colonized parts of the world is echoed by the return of distinctively colonial techniques of power to the metropole in what Michel Foucault describes as "an internal colonialism" (*un colonialisme interne*).[73]

Sonic *renvoi*, as Nancy reminds us, never return immediately to themselves without difference, distortion, or diversion if only because sound spreads out in space, transgresses borders, trespasses.[74] Following this imperative but without

---

[70] McKittrick and Woods, "No-One Knows," in *Black Geographies and the Politics of Place*, 6.

[71] Césaire, *Discours sur le colonialisme*, 12/35ff., at 21/41; Sartre, "Préface à l'édition de 1961," in Fanon, *Les damnés de la terre*, 28/liv.

[72] Arendt, *The Origins of Totalitarianism*.   [73] Foucault, *"Il faut défendre la société"*, 89/103.

[74] Nancy, *À l'écoute*.

succumbing to the lure of ontologizing sound or of making of listening a transcendental, as Nancy is tempted to do, we might say that sound shatters any simple concept of boomerang, of ban, of *banlieue*. Stuart Schrader notes that, while the typical understanding of the imperial boomerang has the virtue of highlighting the "racial revanchism of empire," it tends to reinforce the fiction of an encounter with the savage other that precipitates the degradation of governmentality in a debased and inherently more violent periphery whose import in turn threatens the purity of the liberal, democratic core.[75] Schrader argues instead for a more multidirectional model that would not risk exculpating imperialism provided that its violence remains "over there." Rethinking the boomerang as sonorous resonance troubles such border-policing, for sound, even when it participates in such regimes, cannot simply be contained or excluded beyond a limit.

The notion of soundstate likewise enters into tension with the topological imaginary out of which Agamben conceptualizes the *état d'urgence*, drawing on Carl Schmitt's theory of the exception, as a zone of indistinction between inside and outside, core and periphery, norm and exception, right and fact, law and life.[76] Hence the *banlieue* is not simply a *non-lieu* or non-place, a *zone de non-droit*.[77] If *ban-lieue* means *lieue du ban, lieu banni*, or even rapper Kery James's *ban des lieux*, it is, in Agamben's now classic formulation, an "inclusive exclusion," included only and precisely insofar as it is excluded. A prominent sociological analysis sees the logic of the ban reproduced in advanced forms of urban marginality associated with "territorial stigmatization" and characterized by a "conjugated segregation on the basis of race *and* class in the context of the double retrenchment of the labor market *and* the welfare state from the urban core, necessitating and eliciting the corresponding deployment of an intrusive and omnipresent police and penal apparatus."[78] The logic of the ban or exception is not simply topological or spatial but always already a question of *sonic* stigmatization – something felicitously suggested by Achille Mbembe's phrase "geographies of infamy" (literally un-speaking) to describe a condition of marginalization extending from the *banlieues* through detention centers and border camps all around the Hexagon to neocolonial policy in *Françafrique* and settler colonialism in Palestine.[79] This resonates with the origin of Agamben's political texts in his earlier analyses of the presuppositional character of language. If the *cités* are banned and abandoned,

---

[75] Schrader, *Badges Without Borders*, 232.   [76] Agamben, *Homo sacer*, 44/37.

[77] Kacem, *La Psychose française*.

[78] Loïc Wacquant's analysis has been very influential ("Territorial Stigmatization" and *Urban Outcasts*, 30).

[79] Mbembe, "La République et sa bête": 178/50.

it is because they are mere *phonē* banished from the *logos*. What is at stake is not soundlessness or even an inability to distinguish mere sound from articulate sense but, as Étienne Balibar's analysis hints,[80] a crisscrossing of multiple intersecting frontier- and border-making logics that extend across local and global scales and sounds.

On the one hand, there is the fragmentation and material scattering of the working classes, the decomposition of organized or institutional labor decried by Wacquant, or the social polarization in the classic political-economic analysis of labor market insiders and outsiders that led social-democratic parties in France and elsewhere to abandon their traditional base in favor of realigning along so-called "values" cleavages. The widespread acceptance of this analysis has arguably resulted in leaving the popular classes *voiceless* in representational terms, consigned to the status of an infra-, a-, or anti-political cry of rage and yet precisely included and contained to that extent as non-sense. On the other hand, as a supplement of this void, there is a melee of sounds whose multiplicity is reduced to an undifferentiated mass of noise. While Wacquant observes that the analytical concepts produced by social science, like folk concepts, actively organize and hence mould the collective perception of their objects, the advantage of the aesthetic or poetic perspective – one that in part resonates with Jacques Rancière's understanding of the political as a *partage du sensible* – is that it focuses scrutiny on the ways in which these soundstates, alongside stereotypical *banlieue* images and narratives, are *fabricated*. It foregrounds their ambivalent status as fictional yet efficacious creations. The consequence, as Laurent Dubreuil argues, is that

> in spite of this tremendous noise, in spite of more and more songs, one-man-shows, movies, memoirs or novels referentially originating from the *banlieue* and poetically devoted to picturing it, the consensus jargon overwhelmingly refers to the silence of the *banlieue*, or, at most, to a repeated and quasi aphasiac cry (*cri d'alarme, cri de détresse, appel au secours*).[81]

Just like the images of burning cars and barricades, a soundstate that merely oscillates between "law of silence" and *cri de détresse*[82] is a stabilization or reduction of sound's impulse to wander, trespass, disseminate, disperse, distort, multiply in myriad reverberations. For some, resistance to this double exclusion entails *prendre la parole* or breaking the silence but, as I have argued elsewhere, it is not enough to speak up.[83] Even when conceived as "speaking out of place," as David Palumbo-Liu proposes in a nuanced reading of Rancière, it is

---

[80] Balibar, "Uprisings in the *Banlieues*": 48.
[81] Dubreuil, "Notes towards a Poetics of Banlieue": 103.   [82] Ibid.: 104.
[83] Waltham-Smith, *Shattering Biopolitics*, 102.

necessary to distinguish *invention* from imitation of citizens' (already recognized) speech.[84] This exposes the contingency of existing distributions of audibility while leaving intact the structuring opposition between voice and cry.

Unlike the shots of spectacular "violence" that photojournalists joust to capture or the gunshot at the end of *La Haine*, my field recordings of protests – by virtue of their durational quality and the method of walking through the crowd wearing in-ear binaural microphones – attest that what is actually occluded in the bid to gather the sounds of anger into a coherent political voice or to dismiss them altogether as irrational feeling is the very fact of sound's impulse to self-differentiate, disperse, trespass. In contrast with the symbolic cutting-off of the May Day *cortège de tête* and the circulation of images of police lines dividing militants from the unions, the recordings capture various sonic rapprochements, even if it would be premature and naive to speak of "harmony." For example, the *gilets jaunes* anthem "On est là," taken up by everyone from racialized activists in Action Antifasciste Paris-Banlieue at the front to young ecologists sounding out their political orientations further back, is followed by the same drummers striking up the rhythm of "Siamo tutti antifascisti" [Audio 6]. Soundstates work to homogenize the complex counterpoint of slogans and demands, of voices young and old, of bodies of different ethnicities, races, and genders, but precisely so as to dismiss them all as *casseurs* or *abstentionistes* who exempt themselves from a democratic system that has already excluded them in advance. Tuning into soundstates as they crystallize and dissolve is a new way of mapping less the geography than the *atmosphere* of both the city and the wider political landscape.

4 Cart-otographies: Soundmapping Urban Political Economies

On Sunday April 10, 2022, the day of the first round of the French presidential election, as media outlets began to report on the noon turnout figures and projections, pundits on Twitter were rapidly searching for a map showing the decline in turnout relative to 2017 by *département*. It was the geographical distribution of democratic disaffection, reflecting an uneven set of political-economic effects, that would be the clearest predictor of the outcome. I zoomed in hastily on IPSOS France's map to see the damage in the most deprived areas of Paris, while nervously glancing at Le Pen's far-right strongholds in the north of the country. Abstention was up across most of the country but the collapse in the *quartiers* not as devasting as I feared. The results released that evening would show increasing abstention but also a robust, often impressive showing for the radical-left candidate Jean-Luc Mélenchon. A significant proportion of

---

[84] Palumbo-Liu, *Speaking Out of Place*, 21–23. For an articulation of Rancière's position, see *The Philosopher and His Poor*, 225.

his voters, of which a sizable though frequently overestimated number had been tactical voters, rapidly transferred into abstention or voting *blanc* or *nul* in the second round two weeks later when faced with a choice that appeared to them both unpalatable and undemocratic – almost as many as were prepared to hold their noses to block the extreme right.

As in 2017, electoral maps for 2022 – of chosen candidate by age, income, employment, and first-round choice, as well as turnout – presented a stark picture of the political-economic forces and divisions reshaping the political landscape in France. Its chief remappings include (1) the collapse of the mainstream center-left and center-right parties, driven by deindustrialization and changing forms of work and to no small degree by the decision of the Parti Socialiste's neoliberal or "modernist" wing in this context to abandon its fragmenting working-class base in favor of a realignment along what political scientists call a "values" cleavage; (2) taking advantage of this situation, Macon's capacity to assemble a new bourgeois bloc of socially liberal, cosmopolitan, pro-European, well-educated, middle-class to affluent voters, now extended in 2022 to more well-off pensioners;[85] (3) the inroads made over a number of decades by the Front (later Rassemblement) National into the rural and periurban working classes, fueled to no small extent by the normalization of far-right views by mainstream political actors like Macron; (4) the gradual emergence of a third bloc of younger, urban, variously precarized and racialized workers, unemployed, and hitherto non-voters coalescing behind the radical-left project of La France Insoumise (now the Union Populaire), whose lack of representation in the second round and struggle to build a broader working-class base across the country is marked by an electoral void reaching 50 percent in some parts of Seine-Saint-Denis and levels nationally that have not been seen since 1969.

The sonorous counterpart to this void is the *cri de détresse* (cry of distress), registered electorally and by media and political elites as silence or politically vacated spaces on the map. Aurality is implicated in these uneven geographies as a crisis of listening – both from above by political representatives, who are then forced to make a show of listening exercises though without abandoning an economic consensus that has dramatically increased inequalities and marginal-ization, and also horizontally as social movements struggle to build enduring alliances on the ground. Soundmapping attuned to political economies, especially in urban areas marked by high levels of disaffection or anti-political sentiment, therefore has the potential to generate alternative cartographies often eclipsed by mainstream political science and media consensus. Despite increasing anxiety

---

[85] For an excellent analysis of the evolving political blocs in French politics, see Amable and Palombarini, *L'illusion du bloc bourgeois*.

about political distrust, the focus of elites has remained on the waning "republican front" against the extreme right and a choice between a neoliberal government increasingly authoritarian in response to the effects of deprivation and racial marginalization and an openly authoritarian candidate who would, if elected, maintain neoliberal economic policies regardless of the superficial weight given to social and cost-of-living issues in her campaign. If democracy is understood as a distribution of audibility, soundmapping is a methodology that can potentially give insight into political impasses and tectonic shifts.

There are, however, no soundmaps in this Element. This is because a sonically attuned approach to political, social, and economic abandonment, as described in the preceding section, demands a radical reorientation of traditional cartography. To describe my practice as soundmapping is perhaps even controversial insofar as it embodies forms of way-making in the city *without a map*. Yet ambulatory field recording, tracing and retracing routes across Paris and its *banlieues*, amplifies and participates in the production of space and of alternative geographies – geographies of exposure to insecurity and violence, geographies of making lives in the crevices and crawlspaces of domination, geographies of resistance and solidarity, none of which are legible to a canonical cartography whose genealogy is inextricable from imperialist projects of mastery, rationality, (dis)possession, and erasure. The paths taken on the streets of Paris, the sounds of resistance captured, and the transcolonial echoes traced in this Element are small steps toward alternative, anti-imperialist cartographies. What I call cart-otographies – practices of mapping by ear and of making traditional cartography vibrate and tremble – represent an attempt at the same time to shift the normative frameworks underlying soundmapping as it has been institutionalized by sound studies as a scholarly field and by associated public engagement programs by museums and other cultural organizations.[86]

Mapping has become a staple part of the tools and methods of the maturing interdisciplinary interstice of sound studies and especially in the subset of work devoted to urban sound, whether in the form of "noise maps" that show the distribution of decibel levels and noise pollution across a city or "sound maps" that plot an archive of snapshot recordings onto geographical space from the scale of the neighborhood to worldwide.[87] The ambition to collect and track the spatial distribution of urban sounds came in part as a reaction to soundscape ecology's original focus on capturing the sounds of "nature" in as pristine and high-fidelity form as possible, a sonic equivalent perhaps to professional landscape photography in which quality of equipment and technical composition are

---

[86] On practices of sound*un*mapping and "decolonial echolocation," see Goffe, "Unmapping the Caribbean."

[87] For a brief survey, see Ouzounian, "Acoustic Mapping."

paramount to the genre. By contrast, collections of urban sounds gathered the everyday, often less than pleasant, even annoying, noises that disturb the lives of city dwellers and yet give cities their sense of dynamism. However, urban soundmapping practices have been subject to critique precisely for reproducing the same values that underpinned the aesthetic moralism of soundscape ecology. Many of these critiques have focused their fire in particular on the crowdsourcing trend within soundmapping practices, whereby citizens are invited to upload their own recordings linked via pins scattered across an interactive map on a webpage, a model increasingly popular for public engagement and citizen science projects. While undoubtedly successful in provoking popular awareness of and interest in sound, such projects often overestimate their own democratizing potential, as Paul Tourle, Milena Droumeva, Jacqueline Waldock, and others have pointed out.[88] Insofar as participatory digital sound-mapping projects call for "favorite" sounds, place an emphasis on featuring the unalloyed sounds of nature, or recommend the use of professional audio equipment, not to mention presupposing digital access, they tend to appeal to the hobbyist phonographer and to reproduce a set of humanist, often colonialist, values that vaunt control of the environment and marginalize sounds deemed disruptive, sullied, domestic, or simply mundane.

As Tourle argues, public engagement projects promoted by cultural institutions such as the National Trust or the British Library in the UK yielded sonic archives that privileged and elevated into a universal representation of place the ear of a leisured middle class, typically engaged in the consumption of natural beauty. The result was not straightforwardly to construct a sonic color-line but to homogenize and arguably to "sanitize" whiteness, creating a "white noise" that drowned out the margins, both of racialized voices and of far-right racism. Tourle observes: "Nowhere ... could violence or anger be heard, and only once did a recording even vaguely hint at the kind of socio-political transformation that has seen far-right political parties gain support across Europe."[89]

Another critical perspective on soundmapping practice questions whether sound is inherently antithetical to cartography's need for stasis, grids, boundaries, and to know "where we are going."[90] Sound, Steph Ceraso argues, is by contrast ephemeral, penetrating, and unconcerned with the boundary between inside and outside. While this position risks overstating, even fetishizing, sound's liberty, and underestimating its capacity to participate in reproducing exclusionary social and spatial relations, it is worth considering to what extent

---

[88] Tourle, "White Noise"; Droumeva, "Soundmapping As Critical Cartography"; Waldock, "Soundmapping."
[89] Tourle, "White Noise": 236.   [90] Ceraso, "The Sight of Sound."

sound is able to get at expressivity "in-between" the gridlines[91] or insist upon the "unverifiable, referentially unstable … the partiality and provisionality of geographic knowledge," even the spectral,[92] and as such to what extent sound-mapping is already a "radical" cartography.[93]

In a variation of this argument, Angus Carlyle argues that "sound might always already be a cartography" but precisely insofar as its affective attune-ment constitutes a tactical countermapping that renders audible what remains stubbornly invisible.[94] And yet soundmaps persist in foreclosing the verticality of mapping or what he calls the "God's Eye View," whose homogenizing effect threatens "to flatten sound into a grid of surface and source."[95] Following Paul Virilio, Carlyle links this omniscient surveillance from an unseen vantage point to a militarization of the aerial view. In his book on atmospheres of sovereignty and protest, Illan Rua Wall contrasts two images of figures addressing large crowds: In one the degree of aerial perspective renders the crowd an inert and undifferentiated landscape in comparison with an omnipotent sovereign, while in the other the viewpoint is among the crowd, surveying the scene over others' heads, similar to how my binaural mics place the listener in the place of a demonstrator in the thick of the action.[96] The aim here is more to map atmospheres as territory. The geographical map, by contrast, has affinities with the CCTV cameras from which protestors in the *cortège de tête* shield themselves with umbrellas as they move along the wide boulevards [Photo 11, which is a color version of Figure 3] – themselves designed by Haussmann to facilitate lines of sight and calvary charges against rioters.

The map's aerial surveillance may be linked to the dronification of warfare and state violence that contributes to the proliferation of spatial peripheries within and without national borders, though Carlyle does not make the link to scopic regimes of colonial power that control unruly surplus populations and produce uneven visibility so as to secure new spaces for capitalist accumulation.[97] In a similar way, technologies of the voice at the heart of European conceptions of democracy and humanism rely on a panacousticism that produces unequal distributions of audibility, ensuring that the colonized are at once silent and too noisy, much as the imperialist cartographic imaginary situates *indigènes* as either fixed to an empty wasteland or too itinerant to develop the land. Since the nineteenth century Algiers was a laboratory for the militarization of urban design and governmen-tality in Paris, and for the map as an instrument for making dense, maze-like urban popular quarters like the *kasbah* more amenable to military rationality.

---

[91] Anderson, "Soundmapping beyond the Grid."   [92] Gallagher, "Sounding Ruins."
[93] Droumeva, "Soundmapping As Critical Cartography": 337.
[94] Carlyle, "The God's Eye," 141.   [95] Ibid., 147.   [96] Wall, *Law and Disorder*, 121–22.
[97] Akhter, "The Proliferation of Peripheries."

Figure 3 Marche pour le futur, April 9, 2022, Boulevard Beaumarchais

The task of a counter-cart-otography of (post)colonial Paris is not simply to reclaim and inhabit Cartesian spaces, which my fieldwork experience suggests requires considerable tactical expertise when confronted with the highly militarized French police. Nor is it to celebrate the unchartable aspects of the urban fabric, although there are powerful literary and filmic depictions of women of color re-routing the city and I have observed militants exploit more favorable terrain in Ménilmontant, for example, to lure the police into games of cat-and-mouse. Rather, the aim is to expose and denaturalize the political economies that produce the *banlieues* as sonic *terrae nullius*. At the same time, such cart-otographies have the potential to underscore the resonances between racialized peoples subjected to spatial dispossession and alienation around the world. Sound, I will argue, has the potential to forge what Françoise Vergès describes as "a solid cartography" that mixes historicopolitical and personal spatial memories and draws lines between local cartographies of resistance and "the world of solidarity routes among anti-imperialist movements of the various Souths" and "a millenary site of exchanges" across the Indian Ocean between Asia and Africa, between Muslim and other non-Christian worlds, forming multiple and themselves multidimensional mappings to counter the "mutilated and mutilating cartography" of European imperialism.[98] Against the geographies of accumulation that forge totalities at the expense of

---

[98] Vergès, "Like a Riot." On the "Southification" of the *banlieues*, note their inclusion as the sole exemplar from Europe or North America in a volume thinking sound from/in the South: Steingo and Sykes (eds.), *Remapping Sound Studies*, 4.

producing multiple Souths – both in the Global South and in "Southified" spaces within the Global North – as leftover wastelands for dumping capital's toxic refuse, these countermappings of forgotten, unheard lives are often carved out through creative or aesthetic practices of literature, images, music, and soundmaking.

It is not, however, simply a matter of collecting these treasures to fill the lacunae of the archive. Like the practices of ethnographic phonography and of cultural conservation and cataloguing more broadly, mapping cannot be extricated cleanly from its imperialist genealogy, and one of the ways by which it exercises domination is to decontextualize the represented moment – or perhaps better, the moment of representation – from a broader array of histories, geographies, and phenomenologies. In the work of forensic architecture, sound-mapping becomes a useful counterforensic tool to reconnect the indivisible split second – of a police officer's fatal decision, say, that his defense lawyer seeks to cut out of time – to the unfolding of temporalities and histories of violence and self-defense, of slavery and colonization, and to a wider array of spaces spanning the plantation, the hold of the ship, the settlement, the ghetto, the middle passage, the *banlieue*. To rework Eyal Weizman's comments about the Bedouins, in the moment of no duration, the *banlieusards* are violent delinquents, Islamist terrorists, or oppressed women without agency, eliding everything that the long duration produced and that erupts in that moment.

I became interested in the contradictory notion of the sonic snapshot – short fragments of audio I often paired with photographic stills for installations, not to reduce sound's unfolding but to exploit antagonisms of narrative and affect between and within both "shots" to disrupt any totality of perception. It seemed to me that even or especially in its snapshot form sound more acutely indexes the irreducible *prostheticity* of listening, with or without the prostheses of the field recorder and the microphone – by which I mean, following David Wills, the complex and entangled relay of articulations logically (though not necessarily temporal) prior to and cutting across any solipsistic subject, sensory perception, or secure boundary between inside and outside.[99] In particular, by using in-ear binaural microphones, embodied listening is inscribed in the recordings, making clear that to listen to them is already to overhear someone else's listening. Extending Wills' analysis, colonialism is a technologization that produces listeners and it is this array of sociospatial relations on a global scale – from La Réunion via Algiers or from Minneapolis or Palestine to Paris and back – that is condensed in the sonic snapshot.

That it is impossible to conceive a total representation of capitalism in its imperialist formation is a function not simply of archival erasure but of its

---

[99] Wills, "Positive Feedback."

political-economic composition. According to Fredric Jameson, the spatial segregations it produces both globally and within a city such as Paris prevent the worker from synthesizing the world-system in which his life is inescapably imbricated, even as cartography serves as empire's tool for producing the very invisibility of the other on which the aspiration for totality founders.[100] For Jameson, the resulting fragmentation of the view from above is not to be celebrated but poses problems for politicization and organization insofar as labor is no more able to map socioeconomic relations than the spatial relations key to urban experience.[101] It falls to an aesthetic of cognitive mapping – which I take to include "mapping by ear" – to register and force into the open the uneven (in)audibilities insofar as they express how crises of overaccumulation precipitate spatial displacement and dispossession, whence the restructuring of Paris to accommodate large numbers of impoverished workers under conditions of social apartheid. Reflecting on the representational quandaries posed by Jameson, Alberto Toscano and Jeff Kinkle propose that the intellectual replace the aerial view with Sartrean "tilt-shot" in which he is seen, as from below, as a statue on an oppressive pedestal weighing down on the popular classes with no pretense to mutual recognition.[102]

Yet it is important to avoid homogenizing or identifying with even a distorting and denaturalizating perspective, for neither oppression nor resistance are uniform. I follow Katherine McKittrick in her mixing of Glissant's "poetics of landscape" with Sylvia Wynter's "demonic grounds" to draw upon a grammar of Black-feminist geographies that opens up the possibility of mapping from no unitary or stable vantage point.[103] In the paths that I take to compose recordings in the field [Audio 7] I seek to give myself over to the sensory disorientation of being in the thick of the crowd's turbulent atmosphere and thereby to put mapping and routing in crisis, to be buffeted about by Black-feminist practices of fugitivity or marronage that carve out other routes, retreats, and evasions in the face of enslavement and colonial domination.[104] I feel these eddies at work on the body in tension with the *flâneur*'s privilege to wander autonomously with impunity: in the moments, for example, when the crowd spontaneously communicates horizontally and converts to spatial modalities of self-defense and mutual aid when attacked by the police, whose offensives at once throw out white civilizational feminism's veneer of protection and give a tilt-shot of its complicity in making-vulnerable. Walking well-charted and architecturally designed lines across the city – République to Bastille or Nation – the uneven rhythms, surges, and regroupings begin to reinscribe

---

[100] Jameson, "Modernism and Imperialism," 51. [101] Jameson, "Cognitive Mapping," 353.
[102] Toscano and Kinkle, *Cartographies of the Absolute*, 18.
[103] McKittrick, *Demonic Grounds*, 11. [104] Vergès, "Politics of Marooning."

these urban arteries with the "way-making to nowhere" that Hartman discerns in Dionne Brand's *A Map to the Door of No Return* and that admits of no map.[105] "It touches us," muses Hartman, "without fully emerging as an object of cognition." The distances that matter are not those ones finds on maps but the distances at which nonlethal weapons can give rise to serious injury or even death. The lines that direct the body and its movements are not those that go from A to B but the lines of protestors and riot police facing off, mere inches between shouting mouths and visors [Photo 12], a line under constant pressure, or, increasingly present at large demonstrations, the lines of police alongside the length of the march in and out of which I sometimes dart to weave a sonic narrative of the march's composition.

If imperialism and its disciplinary-methodological manifestations cast the audio recorder as a tool for surveying and surveilling, I attempt to make my listening rove within the crowd's heated atmospheres, splicing and evaporating listening *to* into a listening – and (re-)sounding – *with* that disperses and renders murky imperial panacousticism. These are not a "total climate" of anti-Blackness, coloniality, or capitalism, or what Sharpe dubs "the weather."[106] Rather, the paths traced by my body, moving forward, backward, sideways, with, against, and cutting diagonally across the crowd, more improvised than diagrammed, often fleet of foot to avoid stumbling, take my ears to various "microclimates" of sonorous resistance that have the potential momentarily to shift subjection to toxic, unbreathable atmospheres.[107]

5 Bursting the Eardrum: Reverberations of Violence and Protection

I spoke a moment ago of "sensory disorientation." This can arise in the field for a variety of reasons: reverting to walking with the protestors after a spell walking backward in step with the press corps at the head of the march, descending back into the crowd after scaling a bus shelter to capture an overview or the passage of the march, trying to dodge excessive proximity to PA system speakers or lengthy exposure to loud drumming. Like Shayna Silverstein – who turns sensory disorientation into an ethnographic method, making out of the very lack or loss of direction into the path- or way-making of *meta-hodos*[108] – I have experienced a certain bodily disorientation in the context of spontaneous transcolonial *dabke* performances both in Paris and on a memorable occasion where a local shop at the

---

[105] Hartman, remarks in the closing panel at '*A Map to the Door of No Return* at 20: A Gathering,' November 6, 2021.

[106] Sharpe, *In the Wake.*   [107] Sharpe, "Antiblack Weather."

[108] Silverstein, "Disorienting Sounds: A Sensory Ethnography of Syrian Dance Music," in Steingo and Sykes (eds.), *Remapping Sound Studies*, 241–59.

Figure 4 1ᵉʳ mai, May 1, 2017, Place de la République

west end of Oxford Street lent activists use of the sound system in surreal fashion to take over this crowded shopping district with exuberant dancing, singing, and squealing to the sounds of "Dammi Falastini" [Audio 8, Photo 13]. The *dabke* performance in Place de la République ahead of the May Day march in 2017 was, by contrast, more coordinated, the choreography more impressive in execution, but its impact no less disorienting [Audio 9 (listen with headphones to get the full effect), Photos 14–15. Photo 15 is a color version of Figure 4].

Silverstein finds the "empathic kinesthetic perception" and connectedness required to negotiate *dabke*'s complex interplay of rhythm and movement in conflict with her own bodily entrainment as a ballet dancer and desire to visualize and make sense analytically of structural groupings in the music and the steps.[109] Silverstein makes a virtue of the resulting mutual disorientation, reflecting on how it is generative for denaturalizing dispositions and comportments. In a similar vein, I want to suggest that the sonically induced disorientations I experience have the capacity to disrupt engrained structures of knowledge and conceptuality, specifically those of colonialist inheritance. My choreographic clumsiness attests to the fact that, unlike Silverstein, I am no trained dancer. Rather, in crouching down and rapidly scuttling across the ground chasing sounds and shots of the foot stomps, to see and hear the celebration of transcolonial solidarity and resistance as a literal tilt-shot from below, it was my comportment as a *flâneur*, as a free observer at once

---

[109] Ibid., 252–53.

amid and detached from the crowd, that was put under the microscope and tentatively remodeled. In a different way, at a demonstration in Paris during COP21 I recorded and photographed an elaborately staged yet muted XR chore-ography with protestors initially seated silently at the edges of large-format banners unfurled on the ground for the benefit of the aerial view. As I moved as discreetly and quietly as possible from one crouched or kneeling position to another, my body, its muscles, and its disposition intruded [Audio10, Photos 16–17].

The experience, however, that is most acutely disorienting is no happenstance effect of swirling and noisy crowds or of a collective vigil – that is, of solidary power – but is precisely calculated to have that effect on the crowd at the mercy of (post)colonial domination. What used to send the unseasoned aural *flâneur* spin-ning and still sometimes throws her through a loop are the police offensives, especially aggressive in France and frequently gratuitous, in particular the use of eardrum-bursting detonations. This recording [Audio 11] was made not many minutes after the march set off to mark *1er mai* 2017 with a large autonomous bloc at its head in front [Photos 18, which is a color version of Figure 5] of the union sections in a quick change of scene from the carnivalesque *dabke* and testifies to the disorienting effects of sonic violence. Listen closely with head-phones and you can hear my body rotate, dart, and shrink in retreat as police hurl and launch multiple types of grenade that use a mix of deafening shocks and chemical agents to induce confusion and splinter the corporate body of marchers now kettled between lines of police in full riot gear. As women and children huddle in fear, militants in a regrouped *cortège de tête* turn back toward the police throwing fireworks and projectiles [Photo 19].

The TV and front-page images of the march would show spectacular displays of "violence" and "hooliganism" – not an undignified academic drooling from excessive tear gas exposure, too befuddled even to kick the canister back, but a papier-mâché fire-breathing dragon launched toward police atop a shopping trolley (rapidly decelerating, of course), graffitied and shattered windows of capitalist symbols, rubbish bins set alight, against which police kitted out with defensive shields, visors, helmets and vast supplies of "nonlethal" weapons must defend themselves [Photos 20–23]. The sonic record tells a somewhat different story and as such offers itself as a counterforensic correction of sorts. To start with, there is a palpable discrepancy in loudness between the firepower of the police – detonations of GLI-F4 tear-gas grenades and *grenades de désencerclement* (GMD) at over 150 or even 165 decibels ricocheting off the walls of buildings[110] – and the sounds of protestors throwing projectiles or even

---

[110] Paul Rocher catalogues contemporary usage of French police weaponry in *Gazer, mutiler, soumettre*, 47–72.

Figure 5 1er mai, May 1, 2017, Boulevard du Temple

glass bottles. From the angle of the sonic tilt, the force of the state and of demonstrators is patently asymmetrical. One struggles to discern sonic evidence for an angry mob threatening the police, rather than what I came to recognize as a well-worn police tactic designed to make political hay out of the diversity of tactics and to provoke rebukes by union leaders of anti-fascist militancy, thereby deflecting from the structural violence all were there to oppose. Instead, one hears apprehensive chattering, warnings in aid of self-defense – *les flics s'avancent!* – and the symptomatic coughing and spluttering of unbreathably toxic atmospheres.

This scene, which urges European political thought and white middle-class activism to analyze anew the dynamics of violence and counterviolence, of violation and violence, of vulnerability and protection, in (post)colonial contexts, is not especially exceptional in my fieldwork, though the length of this engagement was especially protracted and sustained compared with, say, the more efficient severing of the *tête* in an equally "hot" political climate five years later after the escalating and generalized use of brutal force and "nonlethal" weaponry during Macron's first presidency.[111] On the silent page, I find myself increasingly reaching for scare quotes, substituting for the analytical work the sonic archive does in exposing the contested fictionality of the (post)colonial imaginary. It is *as if* sound were putting air quotes around the spectacularizing media and cinematic

---

[111] See the table reproduced in ibid., 79.

images that stereotypes Black and brown descendants of migrants and poor *banlieusards* as monsters and bandits. I began my fieldwork in 2013 an avowed pacifist interested in the economic violence wrought on precarized women of color and, while I still maintain that the oppressed must fight for peace and I have never thrown a Molotov cocktail or smashed a window, my experiences in a field where the shadow of police brutality is inescapable turned my assumptions on their head and put scare quotes – marks designed to warn off – around "nonviolence" in its civilizational-feminist condescension. It also precipitates the methodological disorientation by which unplanned *auto*-ethnographic reflection erupts under the force of *oto*-ethnography – an altogether more tailspin-inducing experience than watching the shocking videos that now regularly circulate thanks to smartphones and social media.[112]

If sound is often vaunted for its emancipatory potential – and I have leaned into its capacity to drift to draw out aural notions of fugitivity and marronage – my archive of recordings amply attests to the fact that sound is moreover both an instrument and an index of violence. I am far from the first to theorize sound and/as violence.[113] In his study of "belliphonic" sounds in wartime Iraq Martin Daughtry sees an intrinsic affinity between sound and violence: Notwithstanding that sound seems to float weightlessly, its origin in a "moment of forced resonance that precedes, and in extreme cases precludes, conscious recognition" makes it inherently capable of pressing upon, striking, or even wounding the body, as I suggest in my account elsewhere of sound's searing effect.[114] He argues that this impact can be found even in quiet or pacific situations where reverberation still "coerces bodies" into resonant participation. With Steve Goodman, Daughtry hears both sound and violence as "essentially *vibrational*" insofar as they forcibly disturb a state or system.[115]

This is not, however, to assert an equivalence of violence or its perceptibility:

> The potential for effective censure to follow an incident labeled "violent" is determined by the breadth, prestige, and collective audibility of these communities. In other words, if the victims of violence have been robbed of their collective voice . . . their aggressors can easily define the violent act in other, more euphemistic terms: "collateral damage," "targeted attacks," "clean-up operations," "retribution," "noise." Violence is rendered broadly intelligible only when the experiences of victims are filtered through interpretive practices that acknowledge that their rights and their bodies have been violated.[116]

---

[112] David Dufresne, "L'arme des désarmés," in Bentounsi et al., *Police*, 7–35.
[113] See Cusick, "Music as Torture/Music as Weapon"; Goodman, *Sonic Warfare*.
[114] Daughtry, *Listening to War*, 165; Waltham-Smith, *Shattering Biopolitics*, 7–15.
[115] Daughtry, *Listening to War*, 169 (referencing Goodman, *Sonic Warfare*, xix).
[116] Ibid., 168.

Daughtry's observations point to the second blow by which sound participates in violence: namely, in its silencing, which might consist in an erasure
of sonic traces or in their delegitimation as "noise" or otherwise "violent."
The violent disavowal of violence displaced onto the other recalls a set of
colonial reverberations. Despite Daughtry's nuanced distinctions between
sound and violence, the danger in the analogy is that it elides the question of
the (un)representability or (in)audibility of violence that inheres in the (post)
colonial condition. What can sound – and be heard – of violence?

In some elliptical remarks on philosophical listening and marginality, Derrida
points to the irreducible violence in European thought's self-conception as an ear
always attuned to its outside. Like the (post)colonial republican French state,
philosophy can only give itself the illusion of sovereignty and self-identity by
allowing itself to be struck by an exteriority it disavows. Philosophy experiences
this encounter with the other as an eardrum-bursting violence, but it immediately
recuperates this penetration to itself such that Derrida is left to wonder: "Can one
puncture the tympanum of a philosopher [or, one might add of French republic-
anism] and still be heard and understood by him?"[117] One must then consider the
sonic traces of violence and the sonic violences captured in my recordings in the
wake of an imperialist logic of violent marginality and marginalizing violence –
understood in multiple senses as the double violence of a violence that marginal-
izes and is marginalized, and of the fiction of a violence proper to the margins of
the French state within and without the Hexagon.

On the one hand, ongoing and escalating police violence in recent years in
Paris, despite each blow's apparent eventality, can only be comprehended against
the backdrop of the longer historical view presented by Mathieu Rigouste of
techniques of policing and spatial (re)organization perfected in echoes between
metropole and colonial exteriorities.[118] These intersect with the state's claim to
offer (and require) protection from the dangerous popular classes, whose stigmatization as delinquents reproduces the logic of racialization even where it concerns poor white citizens of French inheritance. With the assaults of neoliberal
political economy, the security (of employment, housing tenure, etc.) afforded by
the postwar welfare state is displaced onto an endocolonial penal system of
security that is designed to drown out cries against abandonment of the social
contract and that renders the most insecure even more so. In counterpoint with
this militarization of public order in the *banlieues* is the expansion of a military-
industrial complex from the 1970s onward and the cultivation of a market for

---

[117] Derrida, *Marges – de la philosophie*, I/x, III–IV/xii.
[118] Rigouste, *La domination policière*.

coercive security techniques and weaponry "made in France" for export to new sites of colonial wars and repression of popular uprisings (Egypt, South Africa, Libya, Syria, and the Democratic Republic of the Congo).[119]

On the other hand, the sonic record of contemporary urban violence is situated within a history of collective resistance, often mediated by music from *raï* to punk, rock, and hip hop, since at least the 1980s in Paris with the Marche pour l'égalité et contre le racisme (Marches des Beurs) and further waves of anti-racist organizing in the 1990s and 2000s, not to mention the mobilizations animated by songs and chants in overseas sites of coloniality across the *outre-mer*. The sonic *éclats* of my fieldwork are thus redoubled and interlaced vibrations of coloniality and anti-colonial struggle ricocheting across time and space. One might even, to rework Daughtry, say that colonial violence just is the reverberation of an aggressive sounding out of the audibility that unsurprisingly rebounds in multiple, scattered directions on whomever is in the vicinity – not unlike the ammunition in *grenades de désencerclement*. Resistance is often heard most loudly in its repression, the vibration of those two opposing forces often difficult to unscramble into a logical sequence, temporally or causally. The swirling sonic confusion in the recordings (who is lobbing what at whom?) foregrounds the moral disorientation produced by a punitive carceral capitalism ostensibly protecting women and law-abiding citizens.

When one hears the sounds of explosives, of rubber bullets fired, of batons thwacked, one therefore hears a continuation of colonial warfare as urban warfare – both the war of the state apparatus against dissent and the *guérillas* it provokes re-sounding in the clattering of broken glass, the crackling of fires, and the scuttling of sneaker-clad feet. Yet beneath the deafening grenades, shattering glass, and fizzling fireworks is an altogether quieter and largely unheard continuation of colonial dispossession by other means: via the war on criminality, drugs, and delinquency, in short on the urban poor and racialized, in the *quartiers*. Amal Bentounsi founded the collective Urgence notre police assassine after her brother Amine, running away from an ID check while on day release, was fatally shot in the back in April 2012 by a police officer initially acquitted by a jury but later convicted on appeal in a rare legal victory. She writes:

> There are definitely links between the lived experience of residents of the *quartiers* and the spread of police violence in social movements. But the differences are significant: in demonstrations the strategy of maintaining order, brutal or not, responds to a real or imagined balance of power; the abuses, even when they go unpunished, are nonetheless not invisible,

---

[119] Rocher, *Gazer*, 126–34.

forgotten, nor do they bring shame upon those who bear the brunt of them. In the *quartiers*, by contrast, a brother, a father, a son may be arbitrarily carried away by the frenzy of an agent without it having any kind of judicial or newsworthy consequence.[120]

In short, not all police violence is heard equally as such. In this way audibility becomes imbricated in processes – and is sometimes directedly mobilized – to decide between legitimate and illegitimate violence. Otherwise put, modalities of (post)colonial listening are instrumentalized to draw a (sonic color) line[121] between defensible violence and the acts of those who may not defend themselves from violence without both allegation and injury rebounding on them. Whereas spectacularizing images of the archetypal *banlieue* riot constructed by media and establishment elites muffle structural violence, I am interested in whether sonorous archives may in limited ways undercut or recompose such snapshots of "violence." If aurality may be co-opted by the state to adjudicate on the legitimacy of violence (the wrong accent, too noisy, or conversely too quiet in response to police searches and harassment), it is possible that sonic traces may help to distinguish patriarchal, racist mythologies of violence designed to uphold the existing social order from noisy, militant modes of reactive or preventive violence as collective practices of self-defense invented by communities in the *quartiers* and brought into the streets of central Paris. Sonic analyses not only test and reframe competing claims to be acting in self-defense but moreover offer novel ways to expose the structural violence typically drowned out by arguments over counterviolence insofar as they remain within the framework of legitimation.

Without speaking in terms of aurality, Elsa Dorlin analyzes this economy which, by a carefully graduated metric, distinguishes those who have the right to self-defense from those whose capacity to defend themselves is delegitimated precisely so as to instill a radical experience of defenselessness.

> Our power of action becomes twisted into an autoimmune reflex. It is no longer a question of directly obstructing the action of minorities, as in the case of sovereign repression, nor of simply leaving them to die, defenceless, as in the framework of biopower. It is a matter of *conducting certain subjects to annihilate themselves as subjects*, arousing their power of action so as to provoke them to exercise it at their own peril. It is a matter of producing beings who, the more they defend themselves, the more damaged they become.[122]

---

[120] Bentounsi, "Les méchants," in *Police*, 63 (trans. mine).

[121] I borrow this phrase from Jennifer Stoever, *The Sonic Color Line*.

[122] Dorlin, *Se défendre*; translation by Kieran Aarons of the Prologue: "What a Body Can Do," *Radical Philosophy* 2.05 (Autumn 2019): 5.

Dorlin's argument gets to the crux of contemporary forms of (post)colonial domination: Rather than aim at the legal subject of human rights or create the powerless victim at the mercy of the state's protection, quotidian police aggression in the *quartiers* and increasingly at protests targets and arouses a "capacity to (re)act" so as to subdue it.[123] This double bind is somewhat distinct from those found in other forms of testimonial injustice whereby one cannot testify at once to the damage and the silencing in that it solicits power in the subject so as to redirect it into (state) power *against* the subject.

A brief survey of the May Day marches that I attended in 2017–22 illustrates how police and protestor tactics evolve dialectically. Since the series of increasingly militant actions in 2016 in protest against the *Loi Travail*, a new typography of street protest emerged, including notably the formation of *cortège de tête*, an autonomous bloc in front of traditional union trucks and a corresponding propaganda war in the days beforehand with state mouthpieces warning in advance of *"casseurs"* planning to attack capitalist symbols, checks and searches to remove not only anything that might be used as a weapon but also medical supplies, and cancelling the traditional tributary marches, while alternative independent media posted often satirical counterstatements. While multiple small affinity groups of autonomist and anarchist activists prepared for militant tactics make up a substantial part of the *cortège de tête*, it is by no means reducible to the storied black bloc – which is in any event a tactic, not an identity. It also comprises university students, *lycéens*, seasoned anti-racist collectives from the *quartiers* including those who cut their teeth in the march of 1983, and trade unionists – all of whom are no longer content to conform to regulated dissent that fails to disturb the status quo and who are, in the personal account of a group committed to nonviolence,

> attracted by the smell of powder, with the feeling that "this is where things happen" . . . precisely because elsewhere, there is not much going on . . . nothing but a deadly boredom, both politically and philosophically . . . saturated with trucks, sound systems, a technical power that crushes all life and reduces demonstrations to, at best, a nice walk, at worst, a funeral march.[124]

The recordings tell fascinating stories about how in large marches where tactical preparation and coordination are challenging due to sheer size and social media surveillance demonstrators engage in experiments to avoid police traps. On May Day 2016 the police had successfully implemented their counterstrategy of cutting off the head of the march, as they would do again in 2022, relying on assistance from the security services of the main CGT union (which has

---

[123] Ibid., 6/3.

[124] "Nous, non-violent.e.s dans le cortège de tête . . .," *Paris-Luttes.info*, May 10, 2018, paris-luttes.info/nous-non-violent-e-s-dans-le-10178?lang=fr.

historically worked constructively with police on crowd control) so as to create a distinction between legitimate and illegitimate protestors. However, those who had simply intended to join the traditional union demonstrations, including elderly people and families with children, became inadvertently caught up at the head of the procession; their shocking induction to police brutality would spur their radicalization and anger other demonstrators.

In 2017 the police did not hesitate to cast a net around the autonomous bloc within minutes of departure, taking an odd projectile as a pretext to deploy first tear gas, then flash and sting-ball grenades as some in the crowd responded by throwing stones, Molotov cocktails, and fireworks [Audio 11, Photo 19]. An even larger bloc in 2018 betrayed the stakes of strategic weaknesses as police adapt to protest strategies. An unremitting and tactically crude offensive against every capitalist symbol in the bloc's path – starting with a McDo whose windows were smashed and walls "redecorated" before it was set ablaze with a Molotov cocktail – served to justify severe repression. The situation descended into chaos with activists escaping water cannons by scarpering down the banks of Seine, exposing the futility of unorganized frustration, and the unions initially taking another route agreed with police before the procession fizzled out. Sometimes there is a struggle to take the head of the march and while anarchists have gradually welcomed radicalized *gilets jaunes* into the bloc and built barricades alongside them (while throwing out any carrying pro-RN slogans), on the Marche pour le futur in April 2022 there were multiple pauses and attempts to regroup the front lines ahead of more mainstream environmental and labor groups as anti-fascists and *gilets jaunes* jostled to dictate tactics and argue with photographers [Audio 12, Photo 24]. For the most part since spring 2019, anarchist and anti-fascist militants have advocated agility, mobility, flexibility, and surprise over mass frontal confrontation, including *manifs sauvages* outside official perimeters. The appointment in March 2019 of Didier Lallement as Préfet de police de Paris, after he had been denounced by a Bordeaux civil liberties association for his use of illegal means to escalate tensions with protestors, signaled intensifying repression, including selecting route destinations suitable for mass kettling and gassing.

Autoprotective repertoires are critical in both contexts, though harder to parse in the sonic archive. In 2017 as I was pulled away just in time to avoid injury, I was unapologetically presented with a choice by the two men clad in black who had come to my aid and the field medic who had checked I was okay: Go back to the unionists with their reggaeton-blasting floats [Audio 13] or the Internationale [Audio 14] and have a good day out or stay and commit to collective self-protection ("you don't have to break any windows," they chuckled).[125] Unable

---

[125] For their security, I do not publish the recording with their voices in the accompanying audio archive.

to sever the head cleanly, the police pushed the dense crowd under a barrage of nonlethal weapons onward to Bastille where they were kettled, drenched in tear gas, and subjected to sound grenades. From that point on my field kit included – besides Zoom recorder, mics, windshields, camera body, and lenses – saline solution, goggles, a vinegar-soaked bandana, and later a gas mask, though I hesitated to add a more conspicuous tactical bump helmet. My apprenticeship extended to reading the mood, anticipating police moves, and taking in fragments of spontaneous popular education or fierce debates about tactics.

Under these conditions of fear of the police and nonlethal weapons, as Rocher notes, "the apprenticeship of demonstrators is very rapid, even without prior militant experience."[126] The experience of numerous *gilets jaunes* awakened to their first taste of police brutality, not dissimilar from my own initiation, attests to the spontaneous transmissibility of popular self-protection in the heat of the moment. In the point of clarification prefixing the English edition of their text in 2009, Le comité invisible uses the metaphors of music and resonance to describe how an insurrectionary movement takes shape:

> Revolutionary movements do not spread by contamination but by *resonance*. Something that is constituted here resonates with the shock wave emitted by something constituted over there. The body that resonates does so according to its own mode. An insurrection is not like a plague or a forest fire – a linear process which spreads from place to place after an initial spark. It rather takes the shape of a music, whose focal points, though dispersed in time and space, succeed in imposing the rhythms of their own vibrations, always taking on more density.[127]

Le comité invisible maintains that, while empire imposes its rhythms upon the world, "a completely other *composition*" is finding its consistency in spaces such as the *banlieues*.

In many ways, the sounds and movements I have captured point to the muscularity and carnality of Fanonian violence, which he conceptualizes as a reversal of the Hegelian dialectic of recognition that puts the colonized subject in their place. Such violence thus has affinities with Yousfi's appeal, discussed in Section 1, to a *barbarie* that refuses to perform to gain audibility through the ears of the white other but instead simply asserts itself and acts.[128] For Fanon, "the dreams of the *indigène* are muscular dreams, dreams of action, dreams of aggressive vitality. I dream I am jumping, swimming, running, and climbing. I dream I burst out laughing."[129] While Dorlin endorses autoprotection for those left unprotected from state and colonial aggression, she also mounts a feminist

---

[126] Rocher, *Gazer*, 100.   [127] The Invisible Committee, *The Coming Insurrection*, 12–13.
[128] Yousfi, *Rester barbare*.   [129] Fanon, *Les damnés de la terre*, 53/15.

critique of the virilism to which movements such as the Black Panthers turned –
what I suggest might also be described as an autonomy of self-defense that
elevates it out of the intimate fabric of lives lived in common.[130] If for Judith
Butler nonviolence is not so much peace, by contrast the peace of which Vergès
dares to dream is not so much nonviolence as a reprieve from the state monopoly on violence and its erasure in respectability politics – a peaceful life to be
delivered through a multiplicity of tactics.[131] Unlike Butler's bid to make rage
articulate – to make it audible to others in a "carefully crafted 'fuck you'" – I am
more interested in picking out what happens when the chants of *"tout le monde
déteste la police," "andiamo," "à bas de l'état les flics et les fachos,"* and "anti-
anti-antifa" momentarily fall quiet and in tuning in to the mutual aid, beyond
a vigilant or "dirty care,"[132] that resonates in the quiet conversations and
inaudible gestures taking place as drumming continues in the distance [Audio
15–17, Photos 25–27]. If for Wall "atmospheres shift the capacity to act" and are
conceived as "intense affective fields" that "seep out,"[133] coloniality's atmosphere of violence operates through not only normativity but what Robin James,
after Ahmed, calls "vibes" – orientations of attunement by which racial, patriarchal capitalism determines horizons of possible action.[134] The sympathetic
resonance of solidary microclimates generates counter-vibes precisely through
spatiotemporal attunements of/to disorientation that refuse the (post)colonial
(dis)alignments The seemingly disorienting audiovisual spectacle of tactical
property damage in fact aims to overturn a structural disorientation or misdir-
ection that marks social rebellion as ungovernable so as to render inaudible the
real ungovernability of capital and its myriad everyday violences.[135]

6 Circulation Struggles: Hip Hop and the *Gilets Jaunes*

The phenomenon (one perhaps cannot say a movement) that is the *gilets jaunes*
has spawned a panoply of chants and songs sometimes with long histories, all
forged under the pressures of contemporary policing.[136] Besides the
Marseillaise frequently sung at the roundabouts, and occasionally the classic
revolutionary anthem "Bella Ciao," a number of singer-songwriters were
prompted to adapt or compose popular chansons. Surprisingly perhaps for
a movement typically presented by elites as rural and reactionary, hip-hop artists
have also been inspired to capture the spirit of the *gilets jaunes*, though there is
little overlap with the rappers who have lent their support to the fight for *justice*

---

[130] Dorlin, *Se défendre*, 133ff.
[131] Butler, *Frames of War*, 182; Vergès, *Une théorie féministe de la violence*.
[132] Dorlin, *Se défendre*, 174–75.   [133] Wall, *Law and Disorder*, 2, 114.
[134] James, "What Is a Vibe?"   [135] Chamayou, *La société ingouvernable*.
[136] On how policing impacts chanting, see Manabe, "Chants of the Resistance."

et vérité pour Adama, for example. A radical-left online magazine dedicated to urban culture, StreetPress, posted a piece in November 2018 on the top five *gilets jaunes* rappers with a somewhat tongue-in-cheek score for militancy.[137] While Kozi's track is dismissed as riding the wave with a score of 5/10, "Blocage" by Mr Fabre, who is described as "angry" and "deeply touched," fares a little better. Kopp Johnson's "Gilets Jaunes" aces it, evincing a guy who has the eponymous protagonists "all figured out," while Momo and Charley's "Ramène la France à la raison" knocks it out of the ballpark, 12/10, and a somewhat wry review: "They are very (very) committed but don't have the voice that goes with it …. All the same, two bonus points for 'immersing themselves day and night' in the *gilets jaunes* movement to shoot their clip."

This rating of militant credentials, which pokes fun at much of the zine's anti-fascist editorial collective as it does at the rappers, is instructive. If placing the *gilets jaunes* and their demands politically has proven intractable to the commentariat and scholarly consensus, French rap has, by contrast, been all too readily pinned down as a voice of dissent emanating from the sociopolitically overdetermined space of the *banlieue* – the epitome of radical militancy. This association of hip-hop culture with urban rebellion only serves to reinforce anxieties about selling out. No less than its American counterpart, French hip hop is, to borrow Graham Huggan's notion of the "postcolonial exotic," "a site of discursive conflict between a local assemblage of more or less related oppositional practices and a global apparatus of assimilative institutional/commercial codes …. Part of postcolonialism's regime of value appears to lie in the very resistance to value," at least according to universalizing codes.[138]

The urge to distinguish between "good" and "bad" rap[139] – either from the perspective of an erstwhile left between *rap conscient* and its commercial imitation or in the pages of the newspapers of reference between respectable and criminalized variants – should be set in the context of the multistranded and nonlinear processes of legitimation and authentication by which hip-hop music has come to ascendency on the Francophone popular music scene through the actions of rappers themselves, as well as actors in the music industries and the political-media commentariat. Karim Hammou argues that, in order that it might circulate as a commodity, French hip hop has, from the 1980s to the present day, been drawn into a set of intersecting circuits governed by regimes of values.[140] The paths on which it has circulated in successive, but also

---

[137] Rémi Yang, "Top 5 des meilleurs rappeurs gilets jaunes," November 29, 2018, www .streetpress.com/sujet/1543510704-gilets-jaunes-rap.

[138] Huggan, *The Postcolonial Exotic*, 28.

[139] See Dalibert, "Du 'bon' et du 'mauvais' rap"; Rollefson, *Flip the Script*, 7–8.

[140] Hammou, "Mainstreaming French Rap Music."

overlapping, fashion include one of aesthetic legitimation that targeted its credibility as an art form, another that cast it as an authentic opposition from the peripheries, and an opportune *Loi Tourban* which imposed a 40 percent quota for Francophone music leading radio programmers to feature more hip hop provided that its more aggressive side as symptom of immiseration in the *cités* were kept subdued. More recent years would see a fusion of the first two strategies such that the validation of an artistic avant-garde came to be predicated upon a sociopolitical posture of resistance.[141] This has led to what Rollefson calls "the paradox of commercialized resistance music"[142] in which the genre's predilection for double entendre and inversional gesture are the only prospect for subverting a routinized and co-opted defiance. For many Booba is merely selling difference, but for others on the anti-imperialist left it is precisely the exponents of *rap conscient* seeking the recognition of a republican state with its fingers in its ears who concede too much. For the right, meanwhile, the Francophone emulation of gangsta rap is decried by Alain Finkielkraut as "a veritable verbal regurgitation of extreme violence" or by Éric Zemmour – the future presidential candidate who would by then be twice convicted of incitement to racial hatred or Islamophobia – a "subculture of illiterates."[143]

What is put into circulation is less a musical creation or voice of the subaltern than a cluster of sonic representations. On the basis of this commodification of the surplus populations in the *quartiers* French rap became a significant segment of the market. By the 2010s and with the advent of online music-streaming services, hip hop had attained dominance among listeners. Circulating on these platforms and on the airwaves is a construction or myth of authenticity by which various scholarly, media, and political discourses "consecrated" hip-hop culture as the paradigmatic expression of the *banlieue* imaginary. The global circulation of French rap, which also gives a certain social mobility to subaltern expression on account of a subcultural or indigenous capital, hinges moreover on a geographical imaginary tied to specific sites: in Paris, *la rue, la cité, la banlieue, le 9–3* (a common way to refer to France's most deprived *département* of Seine-Saint-Denis). Authenticating a (post)colonial collective subject position, the rapper is anointed as the mouthpiece of the *jeune de banlieue*.

---

[141] On the processes of (de)legitimation of French hip hop, see Guillard and Sonnette, "Légitimité et authenticité du hip-hop."

[142] Rollefson, *Flip the Script*, 8. See McCarren, *French Moves*, 6 where she resists the temptation to dismiss hip-hop dance as "'recuperated' counterculture, as a socialist veneer glossing over a capitalist global form, or as miming rather than addressing problems of violence, inequality, and minority invisibility in France," arguing that it has become of a cipher of multicultural France.

[143] Cited in Hammou, "Mainstreaming French Rap Music": 68.

One does hear rap at protests. For example, at the warm-up for the Marche des solidarités contre le racisme et le fascisme on April 16, 2022, blasted out from the speakers was "11'30 contre les lois fascists," a historical artefact dating from 1997 in support of the Mouvement de l'immigration et banlieues (MIR) and released to mark the ten-year anniversary with the first Forum Social des Quartiers Populaires in 2007 [Audio 18, Photo 28]. 2 Bal Niggets and Mystik's "La sédition," which was released on the album *Ma 6-t va crack-er* in the same year and samples American R&B and soul singer Ted Taylor's "Be Ever Wonderful," was up a little later, followed by Keny Arkana's 2006 "La Rage," but rap is far from being the only musical genre espoused by the activists: next up, after a brief snippet of Nina Simone's 1968 Black anthem "Ain't Got No, I Got Life," was Bob Marley and the Wailers' 1974 civil-rights era classic "I Shot the Sheriff" [Audio 19]. Gradually scholarship has come to question this mythology and, in a similar vein to Niang's scrutiny of the *banlieue* imaginary produced in media, cinematic, and literary representations, there is increasing recognition of the fictive character of hip hop's stigmatization or naive fetishization, alongside the complexity of the actors involved in its production and consumption beyond the *cités*.[144]

Like Rollefson, I have little interest in this "zero-sum game," except insofar as the opposition between global commodity and marginal militant vernacular – between circulation and blockage – is already in deconstruction and insofar as analyzing the structural reasons for this conflict can illuminate how hip hop and sound more broadly are implicated in contemporary circulation struggles. It is the refocusing or displacing of politics to the horizon of circulation that links hip hop to the *gilets jaunes* beyond the simple fact that some rappers took the opportunity provided by the unexpected and eye-catching action to lend support or simply cash in. When they burst onto the scene on November 17, 2018, in response to the imposition of a fuel tax, and especially when their actions persisted week after week with unpredicted levels of popular support, the *gilets jaunes* proved difficult for scholars and pundits to parse, as is reflected in the sheer proliferation of think-pieces put in circulation in the mainstream media and on alternative left sites. The working- and lower-middle-class demonstrators, famously gathered at roundabouts in periurban France in their drivers' yellow safety vests, provoked a veritable tide of head-scratching from public intellectuals in Paris and further afield, each able to project their own theories onto the contradictory signals, though not without a measure of consternation. This "noisy" discursive climate would continue to be matched by a wealth of

---

[144] Niang, *Identités françaises*; Hammou, "Rap et banlieue."

sonic production extending from adaptations of football chants and renditions of the Marseillaise to revolutionary songs, popular chansons, and hip hop.

The *gilets jaunes* pose challenges for conventional analyses in at least three dimensions, all of which are variously reflected in the soundmaking practices they inspired: their heterogeneous composition, inconsistent demands, and uncertain organizational form or strategy. The collective actions at roundabouts, motorway tollbooths, and small-town marketplaces, punctuated by more conventional weekly demonstrations in cities, mobilized a fraction of the French population that has hitherto been politically inaudible, drawn from social strata marked by persistent disaffection and abstention. In a flurry of activity, social scientists observed that the *gilets jaunes* compromise blue- and less affluent white-collar workers at small or medium-sized enterprises, less educated parts of the petite bourgeoisie (artisans, tradespeople, shopkeepers, other self-employed small businesspeople), pensioners from similar layers, and those in close proximity to the popular classes, though not the poorest; executives and inhabitants of the *beaux quartiers* are underrepresented.[145] For Étienne Balibar, they are representative if not of current distributions then of a future of "generalized precariousness" toward which France is hurtling under the pressure of wage compression, the decline of trade-union mediation and organizing power, and the increasing intersubjective competition spurred by the expansion of the gig economy.[146]

Debates have raged about the location of the *gilets jaunes* on the left–right spectrum. The occupational profile, cartographical spread, and older age cohort than in recent movements on the left were used to justify their consignment to the right. While it is undoubtedly the case that Le Pen voters are present, they are in the minority and seemingly more audible in online groups than on the ground where trade unionists, *zadistes*, and other left activists have been prominent and popular political education has also been important. On the other hand, commentators were quick to note the absence of the racialized *quartiers* at the start of the action and many rather slow to recognize the kinds of rapprochements with working-class, anti-racist, and grassroots environmental collectives that began to form in cities like Paris, to no small degree due to efforts of Le comité Adama, as discussed in the next section. Also noticeable and promising for forms of feminist activism is the number of working-class women, who have traditionally remained fairly unengaged [Audio 20, Photo 29].

The demands of the *gilets jaunes* have proven no less easy to categorize, being both heterogeneous and frequently contradictory, focused on taxation and purchasing power [Photo 30]. On the one hand, anti-immigrant demands were

---

[145] For a sociological study of the *gilets jaunes* composition, see Bedock et al., "Gilets jaunes."
[146] Balibar, "Gilets jaunes."

undeniably among the various lists that surfaced on social media, but due to strong resistance to hierarchy and conventional representation, the degree to which any of these lists could be said to reflect a consensus is indeterminate and nationalist demands have become increasingly marginal. On the other hand, the absence of wage demands enabled a broad base of support, allowing the *gilets jaunes* to aggregate a wide spectrum of anger and resentment, reflected in the banners and diversity of chants at demonstrations, as well as regional difference. The articulation of the *gilets jaunes* in Paris to anti-capitalist demands and anti-fascist politics is, for example, striking and suitably illustrated by a group of *gilets jaunes* drummers who strike up the rhythm of "Siamo tutti fascisti" after a rousing rendition of the popular *gilets jaunes* anthem, "On est là," thus suturing the yellow vests to black-bloc anarchists in the *cortège de tête* [Audio 5, Photos 31–32]. The yoking of yellow and black was reinforced with the emergence, fairly rapidly in the wake of *gilets jaunes* and formally named in March 2019 but strikingly overlooked by commentators, of the *gilets noirs*, a group of *sans papiers*, and the solidarity collective La Chapelle Debout organizing out of hundreds of migrant hostels in Paris who sought to take their struggle outside of its social and geographical isolation in the *banlieues* by capitalizing on the power of the weekly mobilizations, adopting the symbol of the vest but now "blackened by rage."[147]

The novelty of the *gilets jaunes* is furthermore reflected by how they have resisted canalization into party-political formations. If the actors and demands make for an uncategorizable assortment, there is some coherence around a challenge to representative democracy and the existing social contract,[148] underpinned by a vigorous distrust and critique of oligarchic or plutocratic democracy and a zeal for experimentation with forms of direct democracy, including the signature demand for the *référendum d'initiative citoyenne* (RIC) [Photos 33–35]. The chants and slogans at demonstrations in Paris suggest that those gathered are united by an anti-elite *dégagisme* or specifically anti-Macron sentiment [Photos 36–37]. Besides the cries of "Macron démission," several of the most common chants target the unpopular president personally:

> On est là ! Même si Macron ne le veut pas, nous on est là ! Pour l'honneur des travailleurs et pour un monde meilleur, même si Macron ne le veut pas, nous on est là [Audio 21]
>
> Macron, nous fait la guerre et sa police aussi, mais on reste déter pour bloquer/sauver le pays! [Audio 20]
>
> Emmanuel Macron ô tête de con on vient te chercher chez toi [Audio 22]
>
> Macrons est dégueulasse / Et la police, c'est dégueulasse [Audio 23]

---

[147] Plateforme d'enquêtes militantes, "Gilets Noirs."
[148] Devellennes, *The Gilets Jaunes and the New Social Contract.*

For some, the lack of an ideological formation or political grammar makes appropriation of such populism from below by the Rassemblement Nationale a risk and, for others, the antipathy to trade unions and their conventional organizational structures threatens the longevity and scope if it cannot coalesce into a broader workers' movement. For left populists, a mass movement of this kind, born in the rubble of a labor movement weakened by the atomization of work, requires hegemonizing, but it has stubbornly resisted the seductions of any hyper-leader. The *citoyenniste* suspicion of partisanship and of any political mediation is in some respects a descant to the technocratic reduction of *macronisme* that sacrifices antagonism for a consumerist homogeneity[149] – though in the streets a more dissonant path, often marked by fierce political debate, is pursued. The *gilets jaunes* often appear to be an evental phenomenon with little appetite for movement-building, leaving the task of convergences and alliances to others. At times this is evident in the way the *gilets jaunes* impose themselves choreographically and sonically on a more diverse demonstration – for example, in the simple enunciation of their presence "Olélé olala, quand il faut y aller les gilets jaunes sont là" [Audio 24] or their signature calling card [Audio 25, Photo 38] – and the focus of their tactics against the common enemy of the repressive state, from which experiences of solidarity gradually flow. In actions outside sanctioned perimeters and in building barricades [Audio 26, Photo 39, which is a color version of Figure 6] their burgeoning awareness of collective auto-defense squarely orients itself against the police.

For these reasons the *gilets jaunes* have been analyzed as the epitome of the anti-political tendency sweeping the Global North as distrust of politicians and democracy soars, but there is also a distinctively anti-neoliberal flavor to their attack on policies that favor the rich (of which Macron is an emblem) – so much so that very early on Bruno Amable wondered whether they represented tentative steps toward the formation of an anti-bourgeois bloc in opposition to the twin pillars of authoritarian neoliberalism: the extreme right and the more socially liberally bourgeois bloc consolidated by Macron in the wake of the collapse of the traditional base of the Parti Socialiste and the Républicans.[150] Others have reached for historical comparisons to make sense of the puzzle: Sophie Wahnich, for instance, likens the *gilets jaunes* to the *sans-culottes*, both exercised by inequality across the tax base and the state's deteriorating credibility in a moral intuition of injustice.[151]

---

[149] Hayat, "The Gilets Jaunes and the Democratic Question."
[150] Amable, "Vers un bloc antibourgeois."
[151] Wahnich, "La structure des mobilisations actuelles correspond à celle des sans-culottes."

Figure 6 Marche pour le futur, April 9, 2022, Place de la République

For Joshua Clover, however, there is an interpretative grid through which the *gilets jaunes* become readily legible: It is a "textbook riot," a return after the era of the strike to a variation on the preindustrial bread riot.[152] Like others on the left, Clover's analysis hinges on the vacation of the workplace or factory as the primary sight of struggle in favor of peripheral or non-places, whether the roundabouts of provincial France or the *banlieues* of Paris. In contradistinction to the strike, the riot is a struggle over price-setting rather than the wage, enlists subjects bound by nothing other than their shared dispossession, and takes place in what Marx calls "the noisy sphere of circulation," rather than at the point of production.[153] In a somewhat problematic periodizing gesture that posits a quasi-synchronicity between the phase in the world-history of capitalism and the form that anti-capitalist action assumes, the age of riots tracks to a period in capitalism's meta-cycle in which it is unable to absorb any more labor in the Global North and circulation outstrips production even elsewhere. Clover contends that, unlike the strike, the tactics of circulation struggles – riots, occupations, blockades, looting as ultimate price-setting mechanism – do not have an intrinsic relation to a specific politics, even though, of course, the weekly Saturday demonstrations in large cities assumed a historical form germane to struggles over pay and working conditions, even as the goal of the march up the Champs-Elysées was the siege of the Arc de Triomphe roundabout. In a critique of Clover's paradigm, Alberto Toscano argues that not only is the opposition between production and circulation untenable in contemporary capitalism's mix but also the rhythms of conflict unfold "in conjunction" but not "lockstep" with the cycles of accumulation.[154] Less than a distinct typography or geography, we might instead think of the riot, given the mobility of circulation, as a diffuse atmosphere.

---

[152] Clover, "The Roundabout Riots."   [153] Clover, *Riot*, 122.
[154] Toscano, "The Limits of Periodization."

Toscano complains how the polysemy of "circulation" does a lot of work in welding this schematic together, collapsing critical distinctions between different kinds of "circulation": value in motion, the flow of capital, transportation, distribution, and logistics, the marketplace, the Internet, and so on. Nonetheless, minded to think that the noise of circulation struggles might have the structure of the resonant *renvoi*, I am content to embrace the homonymy so as to make road blockages rhyme with riots in the *quartiers*. The idea of circulation traces a link between French hip hop – less as consumerist materialism or commodity-fetishism than as the *parlure* of a surplus population if not excluded from the wage entirely then whose need to work condemns them to "the most abject forms of wage slavery"[155] – and the *gilets jaunes* who are "without reserves."[156] I thereby seek to draw a line through the *banlieues* and their (post)colonial marginality, tracing the possibility of a new proletarian composition.

Clover argues that as "capital's center of gravity [shifts] into circulation . . . riot is in the last instance to be understood as a circulation struggle, of which price-setting and the surplus rebellion are distinct, though related, forms."[157] To think of *banlieue* rap and the sounds of the *gilets jaunes* as vectors of riot, circumnavigating the circuits of walkable streets and vaporized digital platforms, is to claim that, insofar as they put into circulation commodified representations of (post)colonial subjection, they expose the violence of the state, apostrophized as their antagonist, in the reverberation of their intemperate rebellion. From this perspective, rap's techniques of sampling, which render musical creation in the guise of consumption, exploit musical fungibility precisely in rejecting the regime of private property on which monopoly copyright rests.[158] The sounds of rap and the *gilets jaunes* alike do not so much block the flow of capital as reveal *in their very flow* its blockages and the immiserating release of its pressure valves.

7 Le Combat Adama: Solidary Resonances and Transcolonial Refrains from the *Quartiers Populaires*

Six days after the killing of George Floyd at the hands of police in Minneapolis, Minnesota on May 25, 2020, the police officers who had on July 19, 2016, forcibly held Adama Traoré in a dangerous prone restraint before he later died of asphyxiation were exonerated.[159] The resonances between the two cases – both Black men whose pleas that they could not breathe went unheard – are

---

155 Clover, *Riot*, 26.   156 Dauvé, *Eclipse*, 47; cited in Clover, *Riot*, 160.   157 Ibid., 28.

158 Saint-Amour, *The Copywrights*. On the political economy of Francophone rap and its "guerrilla capitalism," see Silverstein, "Ghetto Patrimony."

159 Le comité Adama has repeatedly complained of judicial obstructionism and interference in relation to expert medical evidence in the case, drawing complaints from four commissioners appointed by the Office of the United Nations High Commissioner for Human Rights about the lack of transparency in the handling of the case. While there has been no consensus on the cause

striking. Adama's sister Assa, who has fought for *vérité et justice* with charismatic courage and persistence in the face of a struggle to acquire credible expert medical reports and constant attacks on her and her family from the apparatuses of the state and the far right, called for a protest in front of the Tribunal de Paris on the evening of June 2.[160] Notwithstanding Covid regulations at the time, a huge and diverse crowd of at least 20,000 descended into the streets wearing face masks. Le comité Adama announced another demonstration on June 13, for which a vast crowd assembled at République but was prevented by the police from marching, as seen in aerial photos.[161] On July 17, two days before the anniversary of Adama's death and the eve of the Marche et Festival Adama in Beaumont-sur-Oise, the *New York Times* featured an interview profiling Assa Traoré and foregrounding both the struggle against structural racism in France and the feminist stance of a woman defending Black and brown men who are most exposed to police brutality in the *quartiers*.[162] On November 26 Assa Traoré was at the front of La marche des libertés contre les lois liberticides as tens of thousands demonstrated against the *loi sécurité globale* and against police violence.[163] In December she appeared on the front cover of *TIME* magazine as one of the Guardians of the Year and as the face of a global fight for racial justice whose echoes rebounded around the world.[164]

All these developments of 2020 I could only observe, due to the Coronavirus pandemic, from across the Channel, following livestreams on social media, on several occasions on my phone while waiting for a parallel demonstration in the UK to begin given the hour time difference. With no accessible field site in which to record, I experimented (albeit without my satisfaction) with capturing my mediated listening from afar. These experiences of connecting anti-racist and anti-fascist protests over broadband networks nonetheless focused my attention on solidary resonances in an era of globalization and digital subjectivation. The "interminable number" of subterranean wires "quivering with different speeds or intensities" to facilitate such connectivity provides

---

of death, a court-commissioned report commissioned in 2021 did find that the actions of the gendarmes were likely to have been a decisive contributing factor.

[160] www.instagram.com/tv/CA2j9pCoXtd/?igshid=YmMyMTA2M2Y.

[161] www.instagram.com/p/CBQ6vKuI1DO/?igshid=YmMyMTA2M2Y; www.instagram.com/p/CBZPp9oI0Sg/?igshid=YmMyMTA2M2Y; www.instagram.com/p/CBYhfg1gdr_/?igshid=YmMyMTA2M2Y.

[162] "Fighting Discrimination, a French Woman Becomes a Champion of Men." *New York Times*, July 17, 2020, www.nytimes.com/2020/07/17/world/europe/race-france-adama-traore.html.

[163] www.instagram.com/p/CIG3Pw-nFED/?igshid=YmMyMTA2M2Y.

[164] Vivienne Walt, "How Assa Traoré Became the Face of France's Movement for Racial Justice," *TIME*, December 11, 2020, https://time.com/5919814/guardians-of-the-year-2020-assa-traore/; Justin Worland, "TIME Guardians of the Year," https://time.com/guardians-of-the-year-2020-racial-justice-organizers/

a metaphor for thinking about the complex "negotiation" and "entanglements" of "different rhythms, different forces, different differential vibrations of time and rhythm" and "intonations" required to knot together different political struggles.[165] Noting these sonic metaphors for mediatization, thinking of negotiations among campaigns and social fractions through the prism of aurality, and specifically wondering what can be *heard* of these tentative rapprochements and uneasy tensions, forces the question of bodies in the street and their reverberant negotiation.

Ethnographers observe that, under the pressures, bodily risks, and visceral densities of the moment, a certain unity forms among militant demonstrators or rioters, bound together by improvised collective action and by a mix of anger and euphoria.[166] Sound is both a trace and an engine of these spontaneous incarnated solidarities. Labor movements with socialist choirs and canonical repertoires of protest songs have long recognized the cohesive power of collective singing and chanting, of which the balcony singing during the Coronavirus has been a timely reminder as it became impossible to assemble in streets and public squares. There is also something galvanizing about the vigorous and sustained drumming that typical underscores and drives forward large demonstrations in Paris. Drummers do not exactly direct demonstrations like an orchestral conductor, but the sounds they make and of protests more generally do provide the electrifying, almost telepathic, conduction that momentarily magnetizes the disparate individuals gathered into an organ or body, large or small [Audio 27–29, Photo 40–42]. This is not to suggest that demonstrations magically disappear political antagonisms but that sonically they are spaces in which both competition for hegemony and attraction to infectious lightning rods takes place.

Writing about the animating prosthetic power of the orchestral conductor, Peter Szendy describes "the *ties*, the *threads* that are woven through and through the conducting and conducted bodies . . . they *are* the reality of bodies that music ties together, assembles, shapes, composes, and deposes. In other words, fictions."[167] In a similar way my fieldwork suggests that sounds can create and remake (political) compositions, apostrophizing demonstrators so as spontaneously to fashion counter-images and configurations to the stereotypes fabricated by the (post)colonial state. In using the term composition to cut across political alliances, soundworlds, and the poetics of the archive, I follow Hartman's idea of a collective Black practice of de- and re-composition.[168] This is, as it were, a resonant poetics of political composition that consists in weaving ties under

---

165 I draw here on Derrida's analysis of the knot in *Negotiations*, 29–30.
166 On the French context specifically: Truong, "Total Rioting."
167 Szendy, *Membres phantoms*, 125/131.   168 Hartman, "Intimate History."

compressed temporalities and spatialities, mobilizing sound's capacity to act on bodies and compel them to vibrate. Deploying Adama's name and those of other victims of police violence within these sonic force fields, embedding them within a roughly woven net of struggles against state violence, has something like this galvanizing capacity [Audio 30–31, Photo 43]. These names and slogans act as a local lightning conductor that restructures an abstract opposition to the weather of racism or state violence into a differentiated, dynamic force field shot through with transversal attractions between microclimates of resistance.

Over the past six years Le Combat Adama has both seeded its impetus within other movements and actions and also served as a centipedal and connective force driving the recompositions of social movements. As well as being hotspots that spark and magnetize energies to themselves, the concrete indexicalities of police brutality also form a braid of names, chants, slogans, and demands that weave together political alliances. In their strategy Le Combat Adama has been fairly close to the logic of *all-iance* that Derrida discerns in the poetics of fellow Algerian-French Jew Hélène Cixous.[169] In her writing, performative and interpellating injunctions constitute an animating power that derives no more from a logic of totalization than from a dynastic power. Rather, these ties and braids, which Cixous also figures as a funambulist's wire or wisp of hair, enable the binding, allying, and even alloying of singularities to one another by rapidly substituting one for another on the spot without subsuming the differences of local and particular struggles. Such processes of sonic re- and dis-placement continually occur in the field of protest as demonstrators hand over the megaphone, one chant eventually exhausts itself in the vigorous collective expenditure of energy or another fizzles out for lack of uptake, or different blocs within a large march create sonic microclimates, sometimes settling into an antiphonal division of labor.

This methodology has a productive affinity with Le Combat Adama's distinctive approach to the question of organization, as Geoffroy de Lagasnerie elucidates in the book he co-wrote with Assa Traoré where he argues that it is as much a struggle on the terrain of social movements and the forms and modalities that elaborate the contemporary social struggle.[170] It rejects the traditional *convergences des luttes* in favor of making alliances with the view to imposing the question of police violence on the agenda of all left movements. If the former descends into the "white-collar racism" of economistic reduction, a crude and atomizing politics of identity, or abstract categories of anti-capitalism or anti-colonialism that reproduce the universalism of the republicanism they oppose, the

---

[169] Derrida, *H. C. pour la vie*, 91/104.
[170] Traoré and Lagasnerie, *Le combat Adama*, 207–13.

Figure 7 Marche pour le futur, April 9, 2022, Place de la République

latter respects the specific difference and independence of struggles when offering support.[171] For these reasons Traoré insists that the strength of their struggle, even or precisely as it assumes national and international proportions, lies in the fact that it departs from the local and is undertaken with all the mothers and daughters and with the youth of the *quartiers* whose voices are unheard.[172] The approach, though, is not merely local but more precisely "transversal" insofar as involvement in the fight for *vérité et justice pour Adama* leads to links with other struggles.[173] This posture has meant Le comité Adama has been proactive in forging alliances between multiple anti-racist, anti-fascist, and decolonial-feminist groups in the *quartiers* and both the *gilets jaunes* and the popular ecologist movement Alternatiba – an open, loose weave gathered only by a common fight against police violence and the unbreathability of the world [Audio 32, Photos 44–46. Photo 44 is a color version of Figure 7].

The listening practices elaborated in this Element and in my practice overlay and illuminate these dynamics of political (re)composition. To put it simply, if political power has typically, at least in European thought, been figured as "voice," then how each voice is heard by another and how voices are heard in concert or discordant antagonism are decisive questions to which field recording can bring a new perspective. As suggested in Section 4, ambulatory field recording, especially with binaural microphones, militates against a totalizing

---

[171] Ibid., 215–18.   [172] Ibid., 203–5.   [173] Ibid., 219.

representation of space and of the city. This form of aural *flânerie* is conducive to moving away from abstract universalism as a mechanism for building new political formations. Mapping these compositions by ear reveals not simply who and which slogans or chants are present but moreover something of the relative enthusiasm, depth, and breadth of participation of different groups, the hegemonies, interactions, and tensions among component parts of the march, and the affective aspects of cohesion and collaboration that show up in different ways when the terrain shifts from discourse and communications to collective action and autoprotection.

A cart-otography of demonstrations moreover points to the presences and absences in the sonic field. Reflecting on the first Marche des Indigènes de la République held on May 8, 2005, two of the organizers make a point of commenting on its sonic composition amid a discussion of historical divisions and realignments on the Parisian left:

> Our songs and music were not "Bella Ciao," the "Chant des Partisans" or the "Internationale." They were the Algerian anthem, the songs of Myriam Makeba, those of working-class immigrants, of undocumented migrants, rap, and songs glorifying the Palestinian resistance. Later, to pay tribute to the martyrs who had been killed in the colonies or by the police, we said prayers and broadcast verses from the Koran.[174]

While this first grouping of revolutionary songs is prominent among trades unionists on 1er mai [Audio 33], they are markedly absent from demonstrations in the *banlieue* where multilingual and international chants such as "Hourriyah, Azadi, Liberté" often predominate if inflected with local color [Audio 34]. The *gilets jaunes* have radically reset the sonic landscape, their popular tunes often hegemonic so one immediately knows when *les gilets jaunes sont là*. Careful attunement to the sonorous field of the *cortège de tête*, which arrives not as a thunderbolt but out of a genealogy of collisions between militant trajectories and as such strongly reflects the evolving reconfiguration of social movements, reveals an emergent composition of *gilets jaunes*, autonomous and anti-fascist youth movements of the center and of the racialized *quartiers*, *lycéens*, and *sans papiers*, as well as radical labor and environmental activists [Photo 47–49]. In May 2018, eager to show their struggle was not peripheral, Traoré boldly called for the *quartiers* to seize the front of an anti-Macron march, along with Action Antifasciste Paris-Banlieue, ahead of the traditional left blocs, including La France Insoumise, raising the possibility of alliances with the Parisian radical left. Eighteen months later Le comité Adama would make another bold call to join the *gilets jaunes* Act III on December 1, 2018 ("Nous sommes 'gilets

---

[174] Bouteldja and Boussoumah, "The Parti des Indigènes de la République."

jaunes' depuis 40 ans"), catalyzing important new alliances between the urban peripheries and rural France and among fractions of the popular classes.

Missing from this mix – an absence accelerated by strategic disagreements over the overture to the *gilets jaunes* – are the sounds of more radical decolonial and indigene autonomy. Assa Traoré's *NYT* interview notes France's failure to come to terms with its colonial legacy. For anti-racist organizers, this represented an important opportunity to bolster transnational solidarities and heighten awareness of the transcolonial violences that proliferate under the conditions of the imperial boomerang. For establishment and right-wing actors the critique of structural racism is nothing but an American import profoundly at odds with the universalism of the French republican ideal and its conception of anti-racism deracinated from its colonial genealogies and subjects. This moral panic about republican values under threat has been furthered by an increasingly reactionary identitarian interpretation of *laïcité* in the service of a nationalist-securitarian project to obfuscate the precarization wrought by Macron and his neoliberal predecessors in both main parties. For those recalling the deaths of the *jeune des quartiers* and shouting "Ni Le Pen ni Macron" in 2017 and 2022 [Audio 35], Macron's scaremongering about "islamogauchisme," "communautarisme," and "séparatisme" was all too predictable, deflecting from the "ghettoïsation par le haut."[175]

Traoré clearly articulates the reverberations between hcr fight for justice and struggles against anti-Black racism in America through the twin genealogies of colonialism and slavery. Yet it is difficult to specify in what sense these transatlantic echoes constitute a *transcolonial* solidarity. Olivia Harrison uses this term to characterize a long-standing multigenerational Franco-Maghrebi involvement with the Palestinian cause dating back to *comités* formed in the aftermath of May '68.[176] She highlights the complex poetic articulation of similarity and difference in this link, taking the example of a song that Franco-Moroccan rap group La Caution were invited to produce for the first album of the Palestinian trio DAM, who are featured in the documentary *Slingshot Hip Hop* exploring the role of the genre in resistance to the occupation. The song's refrain alternates between the groups, switching from Arabic to French: "min ghettos filastin li ghettos faransa / Ma banlieue est lointaine de la Palestine." The moment of transcolonial identification immediately disjoins. The *banlieues* are indeed a far cry from the conditions of the Palestinians in the occupied territories or in Israel. In drawing the analogy – as Achille Mbembe has also done in referring to the "'Palestinization' of the *banlieue*" in which "stone-throwing and

---

[175] For an analysis, see Titley and Lentin, "Islamophobia, Race and the Attack on Antiracism."

[176] Harrison, "Performing Palestine in Contemporary France."

acts of arson in the *banlieues* of Paris subliminally echo the flames and smoke rising from the Palestinian refugee camps"[177] – there is a danger of reduction if one is not careful to observe that the *renvoi* of the imperial boomerang are set in motion from the metropole. In identifying settler or endocolonial territories as laboratories for the militarization of policing, the point is not to make that elsewhere into a source whose conditions of violence, as somehow symptomatic of subaltern resistance and its repression, would contaminate the purity of the metropole or disturb a peace it would otherwise have enjoyed. As Harrison argues, if Palestine has been central to decolonial agendas in Paris such as the Mouvement des indigènes de la république, it is not because of a straightforward ethnic or religious identification. Rather this passage through the transcolonial allows the children and grandchildren of immigrants to make sense of a complex, entangled history of French and British involvement in both the Maghreb and their Middle East mandates precisely to renegotiate their relation to the (post) colonial unconscious [Photo 50].

Le Combat Adama's analytic passes through the Global South but with its own distinctive coordinates, rooted in concrete practical syntheses and geographies, reverberating from *banlieue* to Mali and Sénégal, rather than an abstract South.[178] In a joint interview with Angela Davis, who was quick to express her solidarity for Traoré's anti-racist struggle and to whom she is often compared, the younger Franco-Malian woman charts a different path from the internationalist, Marxist anti-imperialism from which Davis takes her orientation, noting the significance of Palestine for BLM.[179] Both women displace the centrality of Mai '68 in their historical filiations: one onto the Bandung conference of 1955 (echoed in the Bandung du Nord conference in Seine-Saint-Denis in May 2018), the other onto the massacres in Guadeloupe of February 1952 and May 1967.[180]

Le Combat Adama has distanced itself, though, from the radical decolonial and indigene autonomy of the Parti des Indigènes de la République. While members of the PIR have continued to offer unyielding support, condemning the attacks on the Traoré family by "all the 'guard dogs' of the colonial order" (*tous les 'chiens de garde' de l'ordre colonial*),[181] there have also been sharp private critiques spilling into the public sphere. Both are resolutely on the same side against state racism and agree that intersectionality may be used repressively to render minorities inaudible in advance. From the decolonial perspective, though, Traoré's pluralist notion of alliance risks collapsing into republican integrationism, while Lagasnerie suspects the PIR of misreading of Kimberley

---

[177] Mbembe, "La République": 180/53.   [178] Traoré and Lagasnerie, *Le Combat Adama*, 210.
[179] Davis and Traoré, "Rencontre."   [180] Traoré, with Vigoureux, *Lettre à Adama*, 153, 164.
[181] Bouteldja, "En soutien au comité Adama."

Crenshaw, homostatizing categories of race and gender to the point of confusing dominated for dominator.[182] While Lagasnerie has perhaps missed the point made, for example, by Françoise Vergès about white civilizational feminism's complicity with the racial capitalist order of the Global North,[183] debates about the republican recuperation of intersectionality are urgent if it is to be possible to amplify multidimensional resonances in the face of an emboldened authoritarianism on the right and extreme right.

If my fieldwork over the last decade has taught me anything, it is that a white intellectual cannot simply genuflect to decolonial feminism or intersectionality as a moralistic tool of legitimation. Instead of recuperating multidimensional, dispersive worlds of sound and struggle to the rationality of the Western *logos* that divides, opposes, segregates, excludes, it will be necessary to denaturalize, dismantle, maroon field recording, soundwalking, soundmapping, and other aural methodologies and to retune them to the listening and soundmaking practices forged in the daily experience of oppressions disentangleable in their totality. "The challenge," argues Vergès, "is to hold several threads at once, to override ideologically induced segmentation."[184] Mapping the texture of the (post)colonial in Paris in the intermingled binaural difference between two ears might just be one modest step toward that task.

---

[182] Bouteldja and Boussoumah, "The Parti des Indigènes de la République"; see Lagasnerie's Twitter thread starting at: twitter.com/gdelagasnerie/status/1122606860610220033?s=20&t=sB2H5ZE_I4FwEvYfJWyK0g.
[183] Vergès, *Un féminisme décolonial.*   [184] Ibid., 35/21.

Supplementary Material

In order to access the audio and photo content listed below, please visit this title's page on the Cambridge Elements website at www.cambridge.org/9781009054652 and navigate to the 'Resources' tab.

Audio Captions

Listeners are strongly advised to listen to all audio tracks using headphones.

1 Marche pour le climat, 6 November 2021, Hôtel de Ville
2 Manifestation contre l'extrême droite et ses idées, 3 April 2022, Boulevard Voltaire
3 Paris-banlieue contre le FN, 16 April 2017, Rue du Chemin de Fer
4 Paris-banlieue contre le FN, 16 April 2017, Avenue Corentin-Cariou
5 Paris-banlieue contre le FN, 16 April 2017, Boulevard Macdonald
6 Marche des solidarités contre le racisme et le fascisme, 16 April 2022, Boulevard Voltaire
7 1er tour social, 22 April 2017, between République and Bastille
8 Palestine Solidarity March, 22 May 2021, Oxford Street, London
9 1er mai, 1 May 2017, Place de la République
10 Marche pour le climat, 6 November 2021, Hôtel de Ville
11 1er mai, 1 May 2017, Boulevard du Temple
12 Marche pour le futur, 9 April 2022, Boulevard du Temple
13 1er mai, 1 May 2017, Boulevard Diderot
14 1er mai, 1 May 2017, Boulevard Diderot
15 Manifestation contre l'extrême droite et ses idées, 3 April 2022, Boulevard Voltaire
16 Marche des solidarités contre le racisme et le fascisme, 16 April 2022, Boulevard Voltaire
17 Marche des solidarités contre le racisme et le fascisme, 16 April 2022, Boulevard Voltaire
18 Marche des solidarités contre le racisme et le fascisme, 16 April 2022, Place de la Nation
19 Marche des solidarités contre le racisme et le fascisme, 16 April 2022, Place de la Nation
20 Marche des solidarités contre le racisme et le fascisme, 16 April 2022, Boulevard Voltaire
21 Marche pour le futur, 9 April 2022, Boulevard Beaumarchais

22 Marche pour le futur, 9 April 2022, Boulevard Beaumarchais
23 Marche pour le futur, 9 April 2022, Boulevard Beaumarchais
24 Marche pour le futur, 9 April 2022, Boulevard Beaumarchais
25 Marche pour le futur, 9 April 2022, Place de la Bastille
26 Marche pour le futur, 9 April 2022, Place de la République
27 Marche pour le futur, 9 April 2022, Boulevard des Filles du Calvaire
28 1er tour social, 22 April 2017, Place de la Bastille
29 1er tour, 23 April 2017, Place de la Bastille
30 Manifestation contre l'extrême droite et ses idées, 3 April 2022, Boulevard Voltaire
31 Manifestation contre l'extrême droite et ses idées, 3 April 2022, Place de la Nation
32 1er mai, 1 May 2017, Rue du Temple
33 Paris-banlieue contre le FN, 16 April 2017, Avenue de la République
34 Marche pour le futur, 9 April 2022, Place de la République
35 2ème tour, 7 May 2017, Boulevard de Ménilmontant

Photo captions

Those marked with an asterisk are included in the print versions of this Element in black and white.

1   Paris-banlieue contre le FN, 16 April 2017, Le Zénith
2   Marche pour le futur, 9 April 2022, Boulevard Beaumarchais
3   Marche pour le futur, 9 April 2022, Place de la République
4   Marche des solidarités contre le racisme et le fascisme, 16 April 2022, Boulevard Voltaire
5   1er tour social, 22 April 2017, Boulevard du Temple*
6   Marche pour le futur, 9 April 2022, Place de la République
7   Paris-banlieue contre le FN, 16 April 2017, Le Zénith
8   Paris-banlieue contre le FN, 16 April 2017, Rue du Chemin de Fer*
9   Paris-banlieue contre le FN, 16 April 2017, Avenue Corentin-Cariou
10 Paris-banlieue contre le FN, 16 April 2017, Avenue Eduoard Vaillant
11 Marche pour le futur, 9 April 2022, Boulevard Beaumarchais*
12 Marche des solidarités contre le racisme et le fascisme, 16 April 2022, Boulevard Voltaire
13 Palestine Solidarity Protest, 22 May 2021, Oxford Street, London
14 1er mai, 1 May 2017, Place de la République
15 1er mai, 1 May 2017, Place de la République*
16 Marche pour le climat, 6 November 2021, Hôtel de Ville
17 Marche pour le climat, 6 November 2021, Hôtel de Ville

18 1er mai, 1 May 2017, Boulevard du Temple*

19 1er mai, 1 May 2017, Boulevard du Temple

20 1er mai, 1 May 2017, Boulevard Diderot

21 1er mai, 1 May 2017, Avenue Daumesnil

22 1er mai, 1 May 2017, Boulevard Diderot

23 1er mai, 1 May 2017, Avenue Daumesnil

24 Marche pour le futur, 9 April 2022, Boulevard du Temple

25 Marche pour le futur, 9 April 2022, Boulevard Beaumarchais

26 Marche pour le futur, 9 April 2022, Boulevard Beaumarchais

27 Marche des solidarités contre le racisme et le fascisme, 16 April 2022, Boulevard Voltaire

28 Marche des solidarités contre le racisme et le fascisme, 16 April 2022, Place de la Nation

29 Marche des solidarités contre le racisme et le fascisme, 16 April 2022, Boulevard Voltaire

30 Marche pour le futur, 9 April 2022, Boulevard Beaumarchais

31 Marche des solidarités contre le racisme et le fascisme, 16 April 2022, Boulevard Voltaire

32 Marche des solidarités contre le racisme et le fascisme, 16 April 2022, Boulevard Voltaire

33 Marche pour le futur, 9 April 2022, Boulevard Beaumarchais

34 Marche pour le futur, 9 April 2022, Place de la Bastille

35 Marche pour le futur, 9 April 2022, Boulevard Beaumarchais

36 Marche pour le futur, 9 April 2022, Place de la Bastille

37 Marche pour le futur, 9 April 2022, Boulevard Beaumarchais

38 Marche pour le futur, 9 April 2022, Place de la Bastille

39 Marche pour le futur, 9 April 2022, Place de la République*

40 Marche pour le futur, 9 April 2022, Boulevard Beaumarchais

41 1er tour social, 22 April 2017, Boulevard Beaumarchais

42 1er tour, 23 April 2017, Place de la Bastille

43 Marche des solidarités contre le racisme et le fascisme, 16 April 2022, Boulevard Voltaire

44 Marche pour le futur, 9 April 2022, Place de la République*

45 Marche pour le futur, 9 April 2022, Boulevard Beaumarchais

46 Marche pour le futur, 9 April 2022, Boulevard Beaumarchais

47 Marche pour le futur, 9 April 2022, Boulevard Beaumarchais

48 Marche des solidarités contre le racisme et le fascisme, 16 April 2022, Boulevard Voltaire

49 Marche pour le futur, 9 April 2022, Boulevard Beaumarchais

50 Paris-banlieue contre le FN, 16 April 2017, Aubervilliers-Panton Quatre Chemins

Bibliography

Adorno, Theodor. W. "On the Fetish-Character in Music and the Regression of Listening." In *The Essential Frankfurt School Reader*, edited by Andrew Arato and Eike Gebhardt, 270–99. New York: Continuum, 1978.

Agamben, Giorgio. *Homo sacer: Il potere sovrano e la nuda vita*. Turin: Einaudi, 1995. *Homo Sacer: Sovereign Power and Bare Life*. Translated by Daniel Heller-Roazen. Stanford, CA: Stanford University Press, 1998.

Ahmed, Sara. *The Cultural Politics of Emotion*. London: Routledge, 2005.

Akhter, Majed. "The Proliferation of Peripheries: Militarized Drones and the Reconfiguration of Global Space." *Progress in Human Geography* 43, no. 1 (2019): 64–80.

Allan, Michael. "Old Media/New Futures: Revolutionary Reverberations of Fanon's Radio." *Publications of the Modern Language Association* 134, no. 1 (2019): 188–93.

Amable, Bruno. "Vers un bloc antibourgeois." *Libération*, November 26, 2018. www.liberation.fr/debats/2018/11/26/vers-un-bloc-antibourgeois_1694416/.

Amable, Bruno and Stefano Palombarini. *L'illusion du bloc bourgeois: Alliances sociales et avenir du modèle français*. Paris: Raisons d'agir, 2018. *The Last Neoliberal: Macron and the Origins of France's Political Crisis*. Translated by David Broder. London: Verso, 2021.

Anderson, Isobel. "Soundmapping beyond the Grid: Alternative Cartographies of Sound." *Journal of Sonic Studies* 11 (2015). www.researchcatalogue.net/view/234645/234646/0/0.

Arendt, Hannah. *The Origins of Totalitarianism*. New York: Harcourt, Brace, Jovanovich, 1973 [1950].

Arnall, Gavin. *Subterranean Fanon: An Underground Theory of Radical Change*. New York: Columbia University Press, 2019.

Balibar, Étienne. "Gilets jaunes: le sens du face à face." *Médiapart*, December 13, 2018. http://bit.ly/3jM2chp.

"Racism As Universalism." *New Political Science* 8, nos. 1–2 (1989): 9–22.

"Uprisings in the *Banlieues*." *Constellations* 14, no. 1 (2007): 47–71.

Barz, Gregory F. and Timothy J. Cooley, eds. *Shadows in the Field: New Perspectives for Fieldwork in Ethnomusicology* (2nd edition). New York: Oxford University Press, 2008.

Baucom, Ian. "Frantz Fanon's Radio: Solidarity, Diaspora, and the Tactics of Listening." *Contemporary Literature* 42, no. 1 (2001): 15–49.

Bedock, Camille, Antoine Bernard de Raymond, Magali Della Sudda, Théo Grémion, Emmanuelle Reungoat, and Tinette Schnatterer. "'Gilets jaunes': une enquête pionnière sur la 'révolte des revenus modestes.'" *Le Monde*, December 11, 2018. http://bit.ly/3I8RfQw.

Benjamin, Walter. "The Paris of the Second Empire in Baudelaire." Translated by Harry Zohn. In *Selected Writings, Volume 4 1938–40*, edited by Howard Eiland and Michael W. Jennings, 3–92. Cambridge, MA: Belknap Press, 2003.

Bentounsi, Amal, Antonin Bernanos, Julien Coupat, David Dufresne, Eric Hazan, and Frédéric Lordon. *Police*. Paris: La Fabrique, 2020.

Biserna, Elena. "Ambulatory Sound-Making: Rewriting, Reappropriating, 'Presencing' Auditory Spaces." In *The Bloomsbury Handbook of Sonic Methodologies*, edited by Michael Bull and Marcel Cobussen, 297–314. New York: Bloomsbury, 2021.

Bouteldja, Houria. *Les Blancs, les Juifs et nous: Vers une politique de l'amour révolutionnaire*. Paris: La Fabrique, 2016. *Whites, Jews, and Us: Toward a Politics of Revolutionary Love*. Translated by Rachel Valinsky. Los Angeles: Semiotext(e), 2017.

Bouteldja, Houria. "En soutien au comité Adama et contre les coups de pression de la police." Parti des Indigènes de la République blog, June 22, 2020. https://indigenes-republique.fr/en-soutien-au-comite-adama-et-contre-les-coups-de-pression-de-la-police.

Bouteldja Houria and Youssef Boussoumah. "The Parti des Indigènes de la République: A political success and the conspiracy against it (2005 to 2020)." *Verso* blog, October 6, 2021. http://bit.ly/3JVvVPI.

Boutin, Aimé. "Aural Flânerie." *Dix-Neuf* 16, no. 2 (2012): 149–61.

"Rethinking the Flâneur: Flânerie and the Senses." *Dix-Neuf* 16, no. 2 (2012): 124–32.

Brand, Dionne. *A Map to the Door of No Return*. Toronto: Vintage Canada, 2001.

Butler, Judith. *Frames of War: When is Life Grievable?* London: Verso, 2009.

Cadogan, Garnette. "Walking While Black." *Lithub*, July 8, 2016. https://lithub.com/walking-while-black/. Originally published in *Freeman's* 1 (2015) as "Black and Blue."

Carlyle, Angus. "The God's Eye and the Buffalo's Breath: Seeing and Hearing Web-Based Sound Maps." In *Proceedings of Invisible Places/Sounding Cities: Sound, Urbanism and Sense of Place*, Viseu, Portugal (July 2014), 141–52. http://invisibleplaces.org/IP2014.pdf.

Ceraso, Steph. "The Sight of Sound: Mapping Audio." Humanities, Arts, Science and Technology Alliance and Collaboratory blog, October 5, 2010. www .hastac.org/blogs/stephceraso/2010/10/05/sight-sound-mapping-audio.

Césaire, Aimé. *Discours sur le colonialisme*. Paris: Présence Africaine, 2004 [1955]. *Discourse on Colonialism*. Translated by Joan Pinkham. New York: Monthly Review Press, 2000.

Chamayou, Grégoire. *La société ingouvernable: Une généalogie du libéralisme autoritaire*. Paris: La Fabrique, 2018. *The Ungovernable Society: A Genealogy of Authoritarian Liberalism*. Translated by Andrew Brown. London: Polity, 2021.

Cherry, Myisha. *The Case for Rage: Why Anger is Essential to Anti-Racist Struggle*. New York: Oxford University Press, 2021.

Clover, Joshua. *Riot. Strike. Riot: The New Era of Uprisings*. London: Verso, 2016.

"The Roundabout Riots." *Verso* blog, December 8, 2018. www.versobooks .com/blogs/4161-the-roundabout-riots.

Crawley, Ashon. "Harriet Jacobs Gets a Hearing." *Current Musicology* 93 (2012): 35–55.

Cusick, Suzanne. "Music As Torture/Music As Weapon." *Revista Transcultural de Música* 10 (2006). www.redalyc.org/pdf/822/82201011.pdf.

Dalibert, Marion. "Du 'bon' et du 'mauvais' rap? Les processus médiatiques de hiérarchisation artistique." *Volume! La revue des musiques populaires* 17, no. 2 (2020): 83–97.

Daughtry, J. Martin. *Listening to War: Sound, Music, Trauma, and Survival in Wartime Iraq*. New York: Oxford University Press, 2015.

Dauvé, Gilles. *Eclipse and Re-emergence of the Communist Movement*. Oakland, CA: PM Press, 2015.

Davis, Angela and Assa Traoré. "Rencontre: Angela Davis et Assa Traoré." *Ballast* 7 (2019): 44–53.

Derrida, Jacques. *H. C. pour la vie, c'est à dire. . ..* Paris: Galilée, 2002. *H. C. for Life, That Is to Say. . ..* Translated by Laurent Milesi and Stefan Herbrechter. Stanford, CA: Stanford University Press, 2006.

Marges – de la philosophie. Paris: Minuit, 1972. *Margins of Philosophy*. Translated by Alan Bass. Chicago: University of Chicago Press, 1990.

Negotiations: Interventions and Interviews, 1971–2001, edited by Elizabeth Rottenberg. Stanford, CA: Stanford University Press, 2002.

Otobiographies. L'enseignement de Nietzsche et la politique du nom propre. Paris: Galilée, 1984. "Otobiographies." Translated by Avital Ronell. In *The Ear of the Other: Otobiography, Transference, Translation*, edited by Christie McDonald, 1–38. New York: Schocken Books, 1985.

Le toucher, Jean-Luc Nancy. Paris: Galilée, 2000. *On Touching – Jean-Luc Nancy.* Translated by Christine Irizarry. Stanford, CA: Stanford University Press, 2005.

Devellennes, Charles. *The Gilets Jaunes and the New Social Contract.* Bristol: Bristol University Press, 2021.

Dorlin, Elsa. *Se défendre: Une philosophie de la violence.* Paris: Zones, 2017.

Dotson-Renta, Lara. "'On n'est pas condamné l'échec': Hip-hop and the *Banlieue* Narrative." *French Cultural Studies* 26, no. 3 (2015): 354–67.

Droumeva, Milena. "Soundmapping As Critical Cartography: Engaging Public in Listening to the Environment." *Communication and the Public* 2, no. 4 (2017): 335–51.

Dubreuil, Laurent. "Notes towards a Poetics of Banlieue." *Parallax* 18, no. 3 (2012): 98–109.

Dufourmantelle, Anne. *Puissance de la douceur.* Paris: Payots & Rivages, 2013. *Power of Gentleness.* Translated by Katherine Payne and Vincent Sallé. New York: Fordham University Press, 2018.

Durand, Alain-Philippe, ed. *Black, Blanc, Beur: Rap Music and Hip-Hop Culture in the Francophone World.* Lanham, MD: Scarecrow Press, 2002.

Echchaibi, Nabil. *Voicing Diasporas: Ethnic Radio in Paris and Berlin between Cultural Renewal and Retention.* Plymouth: Lexington Books, 2011.

Elkin, Lauren. *Flâneuse: Women Walk the City in Paris, New York, Tokyo, Venice, and London.* London: Chatto & Windus, 2016.

Fanon, Frantz. *Les damnés de la terre.* Paris: La découverte, 2002 [1961]. *The Wretched of the Earth.* Translated by Richard Philcox. New York: Grove Press, 2004.

"Ici la voix de l'Algérie." In *Œuvres*, 305–30. Paris: La Découverte, 2011. "This is the Voice of Algeria." In *A Dying Colonialism.* Translated by Haakon Chevalier, 69–97. New York: Grove Press, 1965.

Fernando, Mayanthi L. *The Republic Unsettled: Muslim French and the Contradictions of Secularism.* Durham, NC: Duke University Press, 2014.

Foucault, Michel. *"Il faut défendre la société": cours au Collège de France (1975–1976).* Paris: Seuil/ Gallimard, 1997. *"Society Must Be Defended": Lectures at the Collège de France, 1975–76.* Translated by David Macey. New York: Picador, 2003.

Gaiser Fernandes, Alexandre. *Everyday State of Emergency: The Influence of French Counterterrorist Security Measures on Public Spaces in Paris.* Berlin: botopress, 2020.

Gallagher, Michael. "Sounding Ruins: Reflections on the Production of an Audio Drift." *Cultural Geographies* 22, no. 3 (2015): 467–85.

Gillett, Rachel. *At Home in Our Sounds: Music, Race, and Cultural Politics in Interwar Paris*. Oxford: Oxford University Press, 2021.

Gilroy, Paul. *The Black Atlantic: Modernity and Double Consciousness*. London: Verso, 1993.

Glissant, Édouard. *Poétique de la relation*. Paris: Gallimard, 1990. *The Poetics of Relation*. Translated by Betsy Wing. Ann Arbor: Michigan University Press, 1997.

Goffe, Tao Leigh. "Unmapping the Caribbean: Towards a Digital Praxis of Archipelagic Sounding." *Archipelagos Journal* 5 (2020). http://archipela gosjournal.org/issue05/goffe-unmapping.html.

Goodman, Steve. *Sonic Warfare: Sound, Affect, and the Ecology of Fear*. Cambridge, MA: MIT Press, 2010.

Gros, Frédéric. *Marcher, une philosophie*. Paris: Carnets Nords, 2009. *The Philosophy of Walking*. Translated by John Howe. London: Verso, 2015.

Gross, Joan, David McMurray, and Ted Swedenburg. "Arab Noise and Ramadan Nights: Rai, Rap, and Franco-Maghrebi Cultural Identities." In *Displacement, Diaspora, and Geographies of Identity*, edited by Smadar Lavie and Ted Swedenburg, 119–55. Durham, NC: Duke University Press, 1996.

Guillard, Séverin and Marie Sonnette. "Légitimité et authenticité du hip-hop: rapports sociaux, espaces et temporalités de musiques en recomposition." *Volume! La revue des musiques populaires* 17, no. 2 (2020): 7–23. https:// journals.openedition.org/volume/8482.

Hammou, Karim. "Mainstreaming French Rap Music: Commodification and Artistic Legitimation of Othered Cultural Goods." *Poetics* 59 (2016): 67–81.

"Rap et banlieue: crépuscule d'un mythe?" *Informations Sociales* 190 (2015): 74–82.

Harrison, Olivia C. "Performing Palestine in Contemporary France: Mohamed Rouabhi's Transcolonial *Banlieue*." *Modern & Contemporary France* 22, no. 1 (2014): 43–57.

Hartman, Saidiya. "Intimate History, Radical Narratives." *Journal of African American History* 106, no. 1 (2021): 127–35.

Scenes of Subjection: Terror, Slavery, and Self-Making in Nineteenth-Century America. Oxford: Oxford University Press, 1997.

"Venus in Two Acts." *Small Axe* 12, no. 2 (2008): 1–14.

Hayat, Samuel. "The Gilets Jaunes and the Democratic Question." *Viewpoint Magazine*, February 13, 2019. http://bit.ly/3Sjp5pC.

Hayes, Nick. *The Book of Trespass: Crossing the Lines That Divide Us*. London: Bloomsbury, 2020.

Hill, Edwin C. *Black Soundscapes, White Stages: The Meaning of Francophone Sound in the Black Atlantic*. Baltimore, MD: Johns Hopkins University Press, 2013.

Horvath, Christina. "Postcolonial Noise: How did French Rap (Re)invent 'the Banlieue'?" In *The Bloomsbury Handbook of Popular Music, Space and Place*, edited by Geoff Stahl and J. Mark Percival, 291–300. New York: Bloomsbury, 2022.

"Quelle place pour les flâneuses dans les banlieues françaises?" *Sciences de la société* 97 (2016): 46–65. http://journals.openedition.org/sds/4004.

Huggan, Graham. *The Postcolonial Exotic: Marketing the Margins*. New York: Routledge, 2001.

Ingold, Timothy. "Against Soundscape." In *Autumn Leaves: Sound and the Environment in Artistic Practice*, edited by Angus Carlyle, 10–13. Paris: Double Entendre, 2007.

The Invisible Committee. *The Coming Insurrection*. Los Angeles: semiotext(e), 2009.

Jacobs, Harriet A. *Incidents in the Life of a Slave Girl*, edited by R. J. Ellis. Oxford: Oxford University Press, 2015.

James, Robin. "What Is a Vibe? On Vibez, Moods, Feels, and Contemporary Finance Capitalism." *Its Her Factory Newsletter*, January 29, 2021. https://itsherfactory.substack.com/p/what-is-a-vibe.

Jameson, Fredric. "Cognitive Mapping." In *Marxism and the Interpretation of Culture*, edited by Cary Nelson and Lawrence Grossberg, 347–58. Chicago: University of Illinois Press, 1988.

"Modernism and Imperialism." In *The Modernist Papers*, 152–69. London: Verso, 2007.

Kacem, Mehdi Belhaj. *La Psychose française: Les banlieues, le ban de la République*. Paris: Gallimard, 2006.

Lambert, Léopold. "Introduction: A Short Colonial History of the French State of Emergency." *The Funambulist* 29 (April 2020). http://bit.ly/3Z5Yoqn.

Lazali, Karima. *Le trauma colonial: Une enquête sur les effets psychiques et politiques contemporains de l'oppression coloniale en Algérie*. Paris: La Découverte, 2018. *Colonial Trauma: A Study of the Psychic and Political Consequences of Colonial Oppression in Algeria*. Translated by Matthew B. Smith. Cambridge: Polity, 2021.

Macfarlane, Robert. *The Old Ways: A Journey on Foot*. New York: Penguin, 2013.

Mahmood, Saba. *Politics of Piety: The Islamic Revival and the Feminist Subject*. Princeton, NJ: Princeton University Press, 2011.

Malabou, Catherine. *L'avenir de Hegel: Plasticité, temporalité, dialectique.* Paris: Vrin, 1996. *The Future of Hegel: Plasticity, Temporality, and Dialectic.* Translated by Lisabeth During. New York: Routledge, 2005.

Manabe, Noriko. "Chants of the Resistance: Flow, Memory, and Inclusivity." *Music & Politics* 13, no. 1 (2019). https://doi.org/10.3998/mp.9460447 .0013.105.

Mbembe, Achille, "La République et sa bête: À propos des émeutes dans les banlieues de France." *Africultures* 65 (2005): 176–81. "The Republic and Its Beast: On the Riots in the French *Banlieues*." Translated by Jane Marie Todd. In *Frenchness and the African Diaspora: Identity and Uprising in Contemporary France*, edited by Charles Tshimanga, Didier Gondola, and Peter J. Bloom, 47–54. Bloomington: Indiana University Press, 2009.

McCarren, Felicia. *French Moves: The Cultural Politics of le Hip Hop.* Oxford: Oxford University Press, 2013.

McKittrick, Katherine. *Demonic Grounds: Black Women and the Cartographies of Struggle.* Minneapolis: University of Minnesota Press, 2006.

McKittrick, Katherine and Clyde Woods, eds. *Black Geographies and the Politics of Place.* Cambridge, MA: South End Press, 2007.

Mechaï, Hassina and Flora Hergon. "'Make Yourself at Home!': The French State of Emergency and Home Searches in 2015–2017." *The Funambulist* 29 (April 2020). https://bit.ly/3KrpDb2.

Moore, Celeste Day. *Soundscapes of Liberation: African American Music in Postwar France.* Durham, NC: Duke University Press, 2021.

Moore, Lindsey. *Narrating Postcolonial Arab Nations: Egypt, Algeria, Lebanon, Palestine.* New York: Routledge, 2017.

Moten, Fred. *B Jenkins.* Durham, NC: Duke University Press, 2010. *Black and Blur.* Durham, NC: Duke University Press, 2017.

Najib, Kawtar. *Spatialized Islamophobia.* New York: Routledge, 2022.

Nancy, Jean-Luc. *À l'écoute.* Paris: Éditions Galilée, 2002. *Listening.* Translated by Charlotte Mandell. New York: Fordham University Press, 2007.

Nesci, Catherine. *Le flâneur et les flâneuses: Les femmes et la ville à l'époque romantique.* Grenoble: ELLUG, 2007.

Niang, Mame-Fatou. *Identités françaises: Banlieues, féminités et universalisme.* Leiden: Brill, 2019.

Niang, Mame-Fatou and Julien Suaudeau. *Universalisme.* Paris: Anamosa, 2022.

Ouzounian, Gascia. "Acoustic Mapping: Notes from the Interface." In *The Acoustic City*, edited by Matthew Gandy and B. J. Nilsen, 165–73. Berlin: Jovis, 2014.

Palumbo-Liu, David. *Speaking Out of Place: Getting Our Political Voices Back.* Chicago: Haymarket Books, 2021.

Parsons, Deborah L. *Streetwalking in the Metropolis: Women, the City, and Modernity.* New York: Oxford University Press, 2000.

La Plateforme d'enquêtes militantes. "Gilets Noirs, pour rester en colère et puissants!" *Vacarme* 88 (2019): 68–79. www.cairn.info/revue-vacarme-2019-3-page-68.htm.

Precarias a la Deriva. "A Very Careful Strike – Four Hypotheses." Translated by Franco Ingrassia and Nate Holdren. *The Commoner: A Web Journal for Other Values* 1 (2006): 33–45.

Puar, Jasbir. *Terrorist Assemblages: Homonationalism in Queer Times.* Durham, NC: Duke University Press, 2007.

Rancière, Jacques. *The Philosopher and His Poor.* Translated by John Drury, Corinne Oster, and Andrew Parker. Durham, NC: Duke University Press, 2004.

Rigouste, Mathieu. *La domination policière: Une violence industrielle.* Paris: La Fabrique: 2021.

L'ennemi intérieur: La généalogie coloniale et militaire de l'ordre sécuritaire dans la France contemporaine. Paris: La Découverte, 2009.

Rocher, Paul. *Gazer, mutiler, soumettre: Politique de l'arme non létale.* Paris: La Fabrique, 2020.

Rollefson, J. Griffith. *Flip the Script: European Hip Hop and the Politics of Postcoloniality.* Chicago: University of Chicago Press, 2017.

Rose, Tricia. *Black Noise: Rap Music and Black Culture in Contemporary America.* Hanover, NH: Wesleyan University Press, 1994.

Saint-Amour, Paul K. *The Copywrights: Intellectual Property and the Literary Imagination.* Ithaca, NY: Cornell University Press, 2003.

Sartre, Jean-Paul. *Critique of Dialectical Reason.* Translated by Quintin Hoare. New York: Verso, 1991.

Schrader, Stuart. *Badges Without Borders: How Global Counterinsurgency Transformed American Policing.* Oakland, CA: University of California Press, 2019.

Scott, Jacqueline L. "Do White People Dominate the Outdoors?" *The Conversation,* October 25, 2018. https://theconversation.com/do-white-people-dominate-the-outdoors-105566.

Sharpe, Christina. *In the Wake: On Blackness and Being.* Durham, NC: Duke University Press, 2016.

"Antiblack Weather vs. Black Microclimates." *The Funambulist* 14 (November 2017). https://thefunambulist.net/magazine/14-toxic-atmospheres/32058-2.

Shehadeh, Raja. *Palestinian Walks: Notes on a Vanishing Landscape.* London: Profile Books, 2007.

Silverstein, Paul A. "Ghetto Patrimony." In *Hip-Hop en Français: An Exploration of Hip-Hop Culture in the Francophone World*, edited by Alain-Philippe Durand, 47–62. London: Rowman and Littlefield, 2020.

Postcolonial France: Race, Islam and the Future of the Republic. London: Pluto Press, 2018.

"A Transnational Generation: Franco-Maghribi Youth Culture and Musical Politics in the Late Twentieth Century." In *Transnational Histories of Youth in the Twentieth Century*, edited by Richard Ivan Jobs and David M. Pomfret, 283–305. London: Palgrave Macmillan, 2015.

Solnit, Rebecca. *Wanderlust: A History of Walking*. New York: Penguin, 2001.

Springgay, Stephanie and Sarah E. Truman. *Walking Methodologies in a More-Than-Human World: Walkinglab*. New York: Routledge, 2018.

Steingo, Gavin, and Jim Sykes, eds. *Remapping Sound Studies*. Durham, NC: Duke University Press, 2019.

Stoever, Jennifer. *The Sonic Color Line: Race and the Cultural Politics of Listening*. New York: New York University Press, 2016.

Szendy, Peter. *Membres phantoms: Des corps musiciens*. Paris: Minuit, 2002.

Phantom Limbs: On Musical Bodies. Translated by Will Bishop. New York: Fordham University Press, 2016.

Thénault, Sylvie. "L'état d'urgence (1955–2005): De l'Algérie coloniale à la France contemporaine: destin d'une loi." *Le Mouvement Social* 218, no. 1 (2007): 63–78. www.cairn.info/revue-le-mouvement-social-2007-1-page-63.htm.

Thompson, Marie. *Beyond Unwanted Sound: Noise, Affect and Aesthetic Moralism*. New York: Bloomsbury, 2017.

Titley, Gavan and Alana Lentin. "Islamophobia, Race and the Attack on Antiracism: Gavan Titley and Alana Lentin in Conversation." *French Cultural Studies* 32, no. 3 (2021): 296–310. https://doi.org/10.1177/09571558211027062.

Toscano, Alberto. "The Limits of Periodization." *Viewpoint Magazine*, September 6, 2016. https://viewpointmag.com/2016/09/06/limits-to-periodization/.

Toscano, Alberto and Jeff Kinkle. *Cartographies of the Absolute*. Winchester: Zero Books, 2015.

Tourle, Paul. "White Noise: Sound, Materiality and the Crowd in Contemporary Heritage Practice." *International Journal of Heritage Studies* 23 (2017): 234–47.

Traoré, Assa and Geoffroy de Lagasnerie. *Le Combat Adama*. Paris: Stock, 2019.

Traoré, Assa with Elsa Vigoureux. *Lettre à Adama*. Paris: Seuil, 2017.

Truong, Fabien. "Total Rioting: From Metaphysics to Politics." *The Sociological Review* 65, no. 4 (2017): 563–77.

Vergès, Françoise. *Un féminisme décolonial*. Paris: La Fabrique, 2019. *A Decolonial Feminism*. Translated by Ashley J. Bohrer with the author. London: Pluto, 2021.

"Fire, Anger and Humiliation in the Museum." In Kader Attia, *The Museum of Emotion*, exhibition catalogue, 86–87. London: Hayward Gallery Publishing, 2019.

"Like a Riot: The Politics of Forgetfulness, Relearning the South, and the Island of Dr. Moreau." *South As a State of Mind (documenta 14 journal)* 6, no. 1 (2015): 26–43. http://bit.ly/3XVm5ks.

"Politics of Marooning and Radical Disobedience." *e-flux* 105 (December 2018). http://bit.ly/3xBrwdo.

"State of Emergency, Curfew and the French Republican Coloniality." *The Funambulist* 21 (January 2019). https://bit.ly/3SfRJHT.

Une théorie féministe de la violence: Pour une politique antiracist de la protection. Paris: La Fabrique, 2020. *A Feminist Theory of Violence: A Decolonial Perspective*. Translated by Melissa Thackway. London: Pluto Press, 2022.

Wacquant, Loïc. "Territorial Stigmatization in the Age of Advanced Marginality." *Thesis Eleven* 91 (2007): 66–77.

Urban Outcasts: A Comparative Sociology of Advanced Marginality. Cambridge: Polity, 2008.

Wahnich, Sophie. "La structure des mobilisations actuelles correspond à celle des sans-culottes." Interview by Joseph Confavreux. *Médiapart*, December 4, 2018. http://bit.ly/3El047u.

Waldock, Jacqueline. "Soundmapping: Critiques and Reflections on This New Publicly Engaging Medium." *Journal of Sonic Studies* 1 (2011). www.researchcatalogue.net/view/214583/214584.

Wall, Illan Rua. *Law and Disorder: Sovereignty, Protest, Atmosphere*. New York: Routledge, 2021.

Waltham-Smith, Naomi. *Shattering Biopolitics: Militant Listening and the Sound of Life*. New York: Fordham University Press, 2021.

Wills, David. "Positive Feedback: Listening behind Hearing." In *Thresholds of Listening: Sound, Technics, Space*, edited by Sander van Maas, 70–88. New York: Fordham University Press, 2015.

Yousfi, Louisa. *Rester barbare*. Paris: La Fabrique, 2022.

Cambridge Elements ≡

Music and the City

Simon McVeigh
University of London

Simon McVeigh is Professor of Music at Goldsmiths, University of London, and President of the Royal Musical Association. His research focuses on British musical life 1700–1945; and on violin music and performance practices of the period. Books include *Concert Life in London from Mozart to Haydn* (Cambridge) and *The Italian Solo Concerto 1700–1760* (Boydell). Current work centres on London concert life around 1900: a substantial article on the London Symphony Orchestra was published in 2013 and a book exploring London's musical life in the Edwardian era is in preparation for Boydell. He is also co-investigator on the digital concert-programme initiative *InConcert*.

Laudan Nooshin
City University, London

Laudan Nooshin is Professor in Music at City University, London. She has research interests in creative processes in Iranian music; music and youth culture in Iran; urban sound; music in Iranian cinema and music and gender. Her publications include *Iranian Classical Music: The Discourses and Practice of Creativity* (2015, Ashgate, awarded the 2016 British Forum for Ethnomusicology Book Prize); *Music and the Play of Power in the Middle East, North Africa and Central Asia* (ed. 2009, Ashgate) and *The Ethnomusicology of Western Art Music* (ed. 2013, Routledge), as well as numerous journal articles and book chapters. Between 2007 and 2011, Laudan was co-Editor of the journal *Ethnomusicology Forum*.

About the Series

Elements in Music and the City sets urban musical cultures within new global and cross-disciplinary perspectives

The series aims to open up new ways of thinking about music in an urban context, embracing the widest diversity of music and sound in cities across the world. Breaking down boundaries between historical and contemporary, and between popular and high art, it seeks to illuminate the diverse urban environment in all its exhilarating and vivid complexity. The urban thus becomes a microcosm of a much messier, yet ultimately much richer, conception of the 'music of everyday life'.

Rigorously peer-reviewed and written by leading scholars in their fields, each Element offers authoritative and challenging approaches towards a fast-developing area of music research. Elements in Music and the City will present extended case-studies within a comparative perspective, while developing pioneering new theoretical frameworks for an emerging field.

The series is inherently cross-disciplinary and global in its perspective, as reflected in the wide-ranging multi-national advisory board. It will encourage a similar diversity of approaches, ranging from the historical and ethnomusicological to contemporary popular music and sound studies.

Written in a clear, engaging style without the need for specialist musical knowledge, *Elements in Music and the City* aims to fill the demand for easily accessible, quality texts available for teaching and research. It will be of interest not only to researchers and students in music and related arts, but also to a broad range of readers intrigued by how we might understand music and sound in its social, cultural and political contexts

Cambridge Elements =

Music and the City

Elements in the Series

Printed in the United States
by Baker & Taylor Publisher Services